An Ordinary Businessman

Bailey Marks

HERE'S LIFE PUBLISHERS, INC.
San Bernardino, California 92402

Scripture quotations, unless otherwise identified, are from the New American Standard Bible, Copyright © The Lockman Foundation, 1960, 1962, 1963, 1968, 1971, 1972, 1973, and used by permission.

Scripture quotations identified LB are from the Living Bible, Copyright © 1971 by Tyndale House Publishers. Used by permission.

Scripture quotations identified as RSV are from the Revised Standard Version of the Bible.

AN ORDINARY BUSINESSMAN
by Bailey Marks

Published by Here's Life Publishers, Inc.,
the publishing ministry of
Campus Crusade for Christ International,
P.O. Box 1576, San Bernardino, CA 92402

ISBN 0-89840-003-1
HLP Product No. 95-00-55
Library of Congress Catalog Card No. 78-71247

Copyright © 1979 by Bailey Marks. All rights reserved.
Printed in the United States of America.

Dedication

To my wife, Elizabeth, who has been to me what I believe God had in mind when He looked at man and said, "It is not good for the man to be alone; I will make him a helper suitable for him" (Genesis 2:18). Elizabeth has had to be more than the ordinary wife and mother, for my schedule has kept me away from home about half of the time, traveling back and forth across Asia. Yet our life together can truly be summed up in the words of our Lord Jesus in Mark 10:7, 8: "For this reason a man shall leave his father and mother and be joined to his wife, and the two shall become one" (RSV).

Table of Contents

Foreword vii
Preface ix
Chapter 1 Life Begins at 31 1
Chapter 2 An Abundant Dimension 11
Chapter 3 Do You Want *Me,* God? 21
Chapter 4 The Most Extraordinary
            Businessman I Know 31
Chapter 5 Check-out for Asia 37
Chapter 6 Multiply and Conquer 45
Chapter 7 An Impossible Dream 53
Chapter 8 Wet Feet for God 63
Chapter 9 When God Opens the Door 75
Chapter 10 One Effectual, Fervent Prayer 85
Chapter 11 Making an Eternal Difference 93
Chapter 12 Vast Work of the Spirit 101
Chapter 13 A Spiritual Epidemic 115
Chapter 14 The Family Business 129
Chapter 15 High Dividends 135
Appendix A The Four Spiritual Laws 139
Appendix B The Spirit Filled Life 143

Foreword

Bailey Marks is "just an ordinary businessman" who, by linking his finite life with the life of the living Christ, has become an extraordinary servant of God.

It is no exaggeration to say that there are few if any individuals in all of Asia who are contributing more to the fulfillment of the Great Commission than this humble servant of God and his associates.

The Christian life is a rich, exciting, fulfilling adventure for all who have discovered the spiritual secrets which are expressed in this book. It is my prayer that you will be challenged and motivated as you read this book to become a vital part of this great adventure.

I am especially excited about this book because I am convinced that there are tens of thousands of able, successful business and professional men and women who, after reading the incredible story of Bailey Marks and the miracle of the Asia-South Pacific ministry, will want to join forces with him in helping to change the world through the power of our living Savior, the Lord Jesus Christ.

> Dr. Bill Bright
> President and Founder
> Campus Crusade for Christ International

Preface

My attention was caught a number of years ago, while still working in my family's business in Birmingham, Ala., by a message at Keswick Bible Conference by Stuart Briscoe, the well-known Bible expositor.

As Mr. Briscoe spoke on the life of Stephen that day, the Spirit of God communicated a great truth to me: *Stephen was just an ordinary businessman like me*, but because he was "full of faith and the Holy Spirit" (Acts 6:5), he was used mightily in the life of the young church.

Now, Stephen was martyred . . . and I admit that martyrdom has never been one of my personal ambitions! But I was impressed strongly that day with the fact that an ordinary businessman, filled with the Holy Spirit and in the hands of God, could accomplish great things for His kingdom.

Many years have transpired since I heard that message. My family and I have since invested the last 12 years of our lives through the ministry of Campus Crusade for Christ International. Time and again I have been filled with awe as I have seen God do great and mighty things through our Asia-South Pacific ministry, which I've had the opportunity to direct. I have continued to consider myself nothing more than an ordinary businessman, filled with the Holy Spirit, but I am involved every day in the most exciting adventure you could imagine!

This book results from the impact that God's Holy Spirit made in my life through Mr. Briscoe's message. It is my prayer that many other "ordinary businessmen" like me will let this account challenge them to see what God desires to do through their own lives, as they are filled with the Holy Spirit and then make themselves available to Him.

Several times over the past few years, various individuals have encouraged me to write this book. "Share your personal testimony and what God has done through the Asia-South Pacific ministry," they have urged. My first response was to laugh! I was not going to presume to write a book about myself! Books are to be written about people after they have passed away. However, I began to find some fallacies to that assumption. Too many missionary biographies have portrayed their subjects as super-spiritual individuals who went around polishing their halos most of the time. I don't believe this was actually the case, nor that those early missionaries would have wanted such an image of themselves presented. So I determined that if my story was to be recorded, I should write it myself.

For that reason, this book is my honest effort to relate how I, a businessman, have responded to what God has done in my life. Some of my responses were positive and others negative. I have tried to deal with the lessons the Marks family has learned together, and how those lessons have caused us to grow in the Lord. It is my prayer that you will find yourself identifying with these situations, and that some of your own spiritual needs will be met as you read about the lessons God has taught us.

There are three major objectives that I desire to see accomplished in this book:

1. That through this account of the working of God in my life and others, many will understand what a loving God desires to do for them, and will come to know Christ as their personal Savior and Lord.
2. That many other "ordinary businessmen" and individuals from all walks of life, who are wrestling with the Lord right now regarding what they will do with their lives, might also reach the point of availability that Elizabeth and I did one Saturday morning in 1967, when we said to God, "Here we are, Lord, send us."
3. That God will be glorified and your vision expanded as you read of the wonderful things our great God is doing in Asia. This book tells not only my story but also that of hundreds of choice men and women who serve God through our ministry across Asia and the South Pacific.

Each chapter of this book concludes with a note of personal application. It is my hope that you will take time to consider seriously these principles and apply them to your own life, because it has been through these same principles that God has transformed my life and the whole Marks family.

Finally, I wish to express my grateful appreciation to five young ladies, staff members of Campus Crusade for Christ assigned to the Asia-South Pacific headquarters, for their assistance in typing, gathering materials and editing. To Nancy Carlson, Shirley Mewhinney, Pat Young, Gail Porter and Barbara Baker, thank you.

Bailey Marks

CHAPTER ONE

Life Begins at 31

The Pacific Ocean was 35,000 feet below; I stared out the window, reflecting on the past as the 747 jet effortlessly pushed its way through the sky. My thoughts meandered around a question posed to me a few hours earlier in the flight by a Vice Admiral in the United States Navy.

Sitting beside the Navy officer on a flight from Manila to Tokyo, I had taken the opportunity to confront the Admiral with the person of Jesus Christ. Although he did not receive Christ that day, he did tell me that he had never before heard how he could know Jesus Christ personally. I responded by commenting that this also had been true of me for the first 31 years of my life. Before I could go on, he asked, rather abruptly, "What's a businessman like you doing in this part of the world anyway?"

It was not the first time I had been asked such a question, and it continues to be asked of me on many different occasions. What *was* a businessman like me doing over in Asia?

Fond memories sifted through my mind of 10 of the most rewarding and fulfilling years a man could possibly experience. Yes, it had actually been 10 years since this furniture man packed up, left his business and became a missionary. There had been times of disappointment and sadness, but for the most part it had been a decade of rejoicing in God.

"If this is a taste of what I can expect from the Lord in the *next* 10 years here in Asia," I thought reminiscently, "I'm not sure that I can handle so many blessings!"

* * *

The story of how I came to Asia began on an afternoon in 1963, when my mother stopped by my office. We were talking about some matter or other when, totally without warning, Mother asked, "If you were to die right now, what would happen to you?"

I remember distinctly the thought that came to mind: "Why on earth is she asking me a question like that?" I was thankful to be standing at the advertising desk with my back to her so she couldn't see the surprise on my face.

Hesitating, I finally turned around and said, "If I died right now, I would go to heaven."

Mother replied, "That's wonderful, Son. How do you know?"

This time I was facing her. I'm not sure what my expression was, but she showed no surprise. I recall being amazed at the reply that came out of my mouth: "If I died right now, I would go to heaven, because Christ died for the sins of the world." That seemed to satisfy my mother on that particular afternoon and that ended our conversation — at least along those lines.

When she left my office, I walked around to my desk and sat there alone. For the first time in my life, I allowed myself to think about what *would* happen if I were to die that very evening on the way home from work. Always before, when such thoughts crept into my head, I'd try to push them out by thinking about other things. It was not pleasant for me to consider death. I believed in God and expected some form of life after death. But to one who believes such things and yet is not sure of his eternal destiny, such thoughts can be devastating.

So my mind dodged away from my personal dilemma to my mother, and I tried to reason what might have prompted our conversation. Why, after 31 years, did she decide to ask me such a question? I had always thought of her as a very religious lady ... always doing good for someone ... always serving on one committee after another in the church ... president of this or that mission home. As we three boys were growing up, our mother's life always centered around us and the church.

Then I thought of my father. He was born into a well-to-do family in middle Tennessee, but because of poor health and other factors, his father lost everything they owned. Dad was never able to go to college because he had to go to work. Being very strong-willed, he set out with great determination to make his own fortune, so that his sons would never have to experience the hardships he had gone through as a young man. He was very successful in doing just that.

As I looked back over my growing-up years, I pictured my father always working and my mother always doing something for our family or someone else. He supported her in her role, and she supported him in his.

Of course, to say that everything was perfect would be misleading. There was a lot of alcohol consumed in our home by my father, which caused much heartache. But even so there was still much love in our home — the love of my parents for each other and their love for all three sons.

My mother's question again claimed my thoughts, and I recalled an automobile accident I'd had a few months earlier. It was a freakish accident, just two blocks away from my home. Someone had been in a parked automobile on the side of the road, and I didn't see him. As I pulled abreast of the car, he stepped out. I swerved and missed him, but unfortunately my car was heading directly toward another vehicle. I swerved to miss it, which headed me for the ditch.

When I swerved the third time, the car shot across the road onto the lawn of one of our neighbors. The grass was wet from a steady afternoon rain, and I was headed directly for an oak tree about two feet in diameter. I had no control at all over my automobile, and the last thing I remember was stomping on the brakes and whipping the steering wheel to the left with all of my might. The tree was coming straight at me.

In the crash, my chest ripped away the steering wheel, and my head went through the windshield. Needless to say, my car was completely destroyed, and I had killed the beautiful oak tree.

"It's me, and I think I'm all right," were my first words to the owner of the tree as I crawled out of the car, which was lying on its side. I discovered that my only physical damage was a knot on my head, a small scratch on my knee and one cracked rib.

Within those few fleeting seconds as I saw the oak tree coming at me, my entire life really did seem to pass before me. I can still to this day remember the pictures that flashed across my mind. I didn't share this with anyone, but some of the pictures were not at all pleasing.

But sitting there at my desk, pondering my mother's question, I still had no solution to the serious thinking I'd done after the accident. "What *would* happen to me if I had another wreck?" I asked myself. "What if I weren't so fortunate this time?" I had no answer.

"I believe in God," I reviewed to myself mentally, "and I believe that God had a Son by the name of Jesus . . . but how in the world do they relate to me?" I had attended church for 31 years, but to my knowledge no one had ever placed God and His Son Jesus in proper perspective to my own personal life.

From that afternoon that one question plagued me continually: "If I die today, what will happen to me?"

Now, one would think that a man of average intelligence who was so bothered by such a question would be able to go and talk it over with his mother, knowing how much she loved him. But that was not my case; in fact, I have discovered that I was really not unique at all to be embarrassed to bring up the subject. Most of us feel insecure and afraid to discuss spiritual truths, largely because we are very uninformed about them.

So I drifted along in my dilemma, talking occasionally with my wife about spiritual things, but primarily just lying in bed at night, pondering my questions over and over in my mind.

I had a working knowledge of the Bible from some high school and college courses, all of which were conducted on an historical basis. But I can't recall ever having the Bible related to the person of Christ, except as an historical man. As a result, I was one of those individuals who thought the Bible was full of fallacies and contradictions. Of course, I would have been most embarrassed if anyone had asked me to name some fallacy, because I had no specifics to back up my assumption.

But my knowledge of the Bible was sufficient to know that a Christian has eternal life. I recall lying in bed one night, thinking through the matter once again.

"All right, Bailey," I told myself, "you are a Christian, and you have eternal life. So why are you so concerned?" My logical mind argued back, "But how — or when — did I become a Christian?" I had no answer. All I could say was that I was born in what I thought to be a Christian home in the Bible belt of the United States, so I must be a Christian.

Again I defeated my own argument with another question: "What could the geographical location of my birth have to do with my eternal destiny with God?" Really, what difference did it make if I were born in the United States or India? Being born in Alabama surely couldn't make me a Christian!

That night I concluded that I was not a Christian. I didn't know what I was, but I knew with certainty that I wasn't a Christian.

About this time, I began to notice something different about my wife.

According to my standards, I have the most wonderful wife in all the world. We have always had as close to a perfect relationship as I think any two people could experience. I fell in love with Elizabeth the first time I saw her as a young lady. I'd known Elizabeth years before, in the role of the younger sister of a good friend of mine. While she was in high school, I wanted to date her, but since I was six years older than she, her mother wisely did not allow her to date me then.

Elizabeth and I met again after I had graduated from college, served two years as an officer in the United States Navy and returned home to Birmingham to enter our family business. We were both waterskiing one weekend at a lake near Birmingham, and I had gone over to join the group she was with that day. As I leaned over the side of my boat, Elizabeth came up out of the water. If you can say that it was love at first sight when a girl's hair is streaming wet and stringy, it must have been — and it was.

Immediately upon seeing her at the lake, I had the confident assurance that she was going to be my wife, and I told her so several days later. It was more than two years before we were married, but from the very beginning of our marriage, our relationship was wonderful.

As a young married couple, our lives were very similar to those of my parents. I was very busy trying to work as hard as my father and become as good a businessman as he was. Elizabeth, on the other hand, was unintentionally imitating my mother. She joined every church group there was and every type of benevolent civic organization. She was the youngest lady to be elected as head of the ladies auxiliary in our church. In her thinking and mine, she was stacking up a lot of religious points for herself.

Then one day I began to notice a change taking place in Elizabeth's life — a good change. I was finding a new quality of life about her that could be described in part as warmth, depth of concern and appreciation for others.

She began to awaken at the same time I did in the morning, propping herself up in bed and reading her Bible. Formerly, she had slept as I shaved and dressed, and by that time our servant had breakfast prepared. Then Elizabeth would join me for breakfast before I left for work. After several days of Elizabeth's new schedule, I recall thinking to myself, "This is just wonderful for the mother of my children to be reading her Bible every day!"

A few weeks went by, and then suddenly one morning I found myself in a very awkward position. I was in the midst of getting dressed, and Elizabeth was propped up in bed reading her Bible. I had one leg in my trousers and the other leg in midair when Elizabeth looked up at me suddenly and said, "Bailey, if you were to die right now, what would happen to you?"

Fortunately, I was standing very close to the bed. I nonchalantly sat down, slipped my other leg into my trousers, stood up and said, "I would go to heaven."

Her next question was, "How do you know?" By this time, I had rehearsed my answer well, so I looked at her and replied, "Because Christ died for the sins of the world."

What else was said I don't remember. But I do remember driving to work that morning and calling myself every stupid name I could think of. For months I had battled this issue in my mind, and quite possibly I could have discovered some answers that morning with Elizabeth — but my pride won out once again. I wasn't going to admit that someone might know something I didn't! So I tried to deceive Elizabeth, just as I had my mother.

Fortunately, only a few more weeks went by until one Friday night Elizabeth asked me to take her to a neighborhood Bible study. On many Friday nights I worked, and on those I didn't, our activities wouldn't have resembled a Bible study group in any form or fashion. But I pretended to be very gracious about consenting to take Elizabeth to the Bible study, while deep in my heart I wanted to attend so badly that I couldn't think about anything else.

Although I was anxious to go, I was also wondering what kind of strange people would be there. As the evening turned out, I was one of the most surprised individuals in attendance! We drove up in front of a very fashionable home, the home of one of Birmingham's leading oral surgeons, Dr. Bill Buck and

Life Begins at 31

his wife, Janie. We walked into the home, and I saw that none of the people had two heads, as I had somewhat suspected they might. The Bible study teacher was not dressed in a black dress with black lace-up shoes, black stockings and her hair up in a bun, as I had expected. Instead she was dressed very stylishly.

As we entered I was introduced to the Bible study leader, Mrs. Elizabeth Newbold. I said simply, "Hello." When we left two hours later, I said, "Thank you very much, I enjoyed the class. Goodbye." I don't recall saying another word to anyone. But between the hello and goodbye that evening, my life was transformed.

There were over a hundred people in that room, but I felt as if I were the only one there, with Mrs. Newbold speaking directly to me. She taught from the book of Acts and discussed one of Paul's missionary journeys. After relating where Paul was going, she began to explain what Paul was saying, and I listened intently. That night I heard some very basic spiritual truths, and as the questions perplexing me for many months were all answered, I fell in love with Jesus.

She explained how much God loved me as an individual. She said that if I had been the only person who ever lived in the history of all mankind, God loved me so much that He would have sent His Son, the Lord Jesus Christ, to die on the cross for my sins alone. Until that time, I had always generalized that "Christ died for the sins of the world." But now I was hearing the message of the cross broken down to a personal relationship between one man and God.

She further explained that I was a sinner. I had no problem understanding that! However, my personal definition of sin was distorted. To me, sin was the more gross things in my life. But she said that the Bible calls sin a heart attitude, and that the gross things I was classifying as sin were the result of the wrong attitudes entrenched in my heart.

Then for the first time I began to understand the significance of the cross. Mrs. Newbold explained that because of the sin in my life, I was the one who should have been required to pay the penalty. But because of God's infinite love for me, He sent Jesus Christ as my substitute, to pay my penalty.

The lights were beginning to come on in my mind when Mrs. Newbold paused and said, "You can believe everything I have said here this evening and be 13 inches away from becoming a Christian." My immediate reaction was one of surprise, because I couldn't understand what 13 inches could have to do with such an important matter.

With a gentle smile, Mrs. Newbold reminded me that this is the approximate distance between my mind and my heart. "You can have a mental understanding of everything that is said here tonight," she said, "but receiving Christ involves a heart attitude, a change in heart. An individual must receive Jesus Christ into his heart and life in order to become a child of God, in order to be a Christian."

My mind is blank as to what happened for the rest of the evening. I was too caught up in thinking about what Christ had done for me. There was no invitation to receive Christ given that night, but my life was transformed. Sitting in the Bible class, I didn't close my eyes, I didn't get on my knees, I didn't even bow my head. I just sat in that chair and prayed within my heart a very untheological prayer: "God, if what that lady is saying is true, if Jesus is the way to know You, then I want Him to come into my life right now." That was all, and yet I left that room with the confident assurance that Christ had come into my life.

It occurs to me that many of you reading this book may find yourselves in the same situation — trying desperately to deceive yourselves and others, but in fact, never having established personal relationships with God through His Son, Jesus Christ.

The Bible says, "But as many as received Him, to them He gave the right to become children of God" (John 1:12). Jesus said, "Behold, I stand at the door and knock; if anyone hears My voice and opens the door, I will come in to him" (Revelation 3:20). God made these promises to you, and at this very moment you can receive Christ into your life to be your Lord and Savior, just as I did that Friday evening in May, 1964.

Since I accepted Christ that night, I've met many people who have started immediately to tell others what has happened in their lives — often within a matter of minutes or hours after receiving Christ. I was not one of those people. In fact, it was three months before I told my wife that I had invited Christ to come into my life.

We continued to attend the Bible class on Friday nights,

and I began to see some growth taking place in my own life. I'm not a very poetic person, but the best way I know to describe this growth is to compare it with a flower's growth. As a flower buds, the rays of sunshine and drops of rain fall upon its petals, and it begins to bloom and grow. I was experiencing this same phenomenon in my own life. I had been born spiritually, or reborn, as the Bible says.

Once I began to talk about what was taking place in my life, I started to realize what had been happening spiritually all around me. My mother had invited Christ to come into her life shortly before she asked me that disturbing question in my office. At the time she had become deeply engrossed in anti-communism and saw no future for the United States. One day while she was expressing her frustrations, someone told her that there is hope in Jesus Christ and asked her if she were a Christian.

Now my mother had walked the aisle at church many times, but she had never by faith invited Christ to come into her life. Searching, she began attending a ladies Bible study conducted by Mrs. Newbold, and there in the class one day she established her personal relationship with God. Her new discovery and concern for me had prompted her to ask me those questions in my office soon afterward.

At the same time, Mother began to "scheme" to get Elizabeth to attend this same ladies Bible study. Afraid that too much mother-in-law influence might cause Elizabeth to resist, she encouraged an acquaintance of Elizabeth's who was attending the Bible study to invite her. This friend called her every week for weeks, until finally Elizabeth conceded to go.

At that time Mrs. Newbold was teaching from the prophetic book of Revelation, and the class was studying the period of time called the Tribulation. My wife invited Christ to come into her life at the first class she attended.

In the family progression, I was the next person to make a decision for Christ. Several years later, my father committed his life to Christ; then my brothers, Elizabeth's brother, and many others among our relatives.

That was in 1964 . . . and just four and a half years later I found myself traveling the skies of Asia.

What is a businessman like me doing in this part of the

world? I'm living the most exciting, fulfilling and rewarding life that one can imagine, sharing the message of God's love and forgiveness and how to have a personal relationship with Him . . . a message that I had to wait 31 years to hear about myself.

Personal Application

Is there any doubt in your mind at this moment as to whether or not you have eternal life?

If so, I would encourage you to turn to Appendix A, page 139, where I have included the *Four Spiritual Laws,* a concise presentation of the gospel that has been used in the lives of millions of people all over the world. It is my prayer that you will read carefully through these pages and invite Jesus Christ to come into your life to be your Savior and Lord.

CHAPTER TWO

An Abundant Dimension

I was exhausted. I boarded an airplane heading home after a long five and a half weeks on the road in six different countries.

From early morning until late at night, my days had been full — giving conference messages, counseling with our staff over ministry decisions, meeting with pastors and Christian leaders, sharing the claims of Christ with scores of individuals. I had loved every minute of it, but it was hard work, and I was tired.

As I boarded the plane, I murmured a quiet prayer: "Lord, I don't want to talk to anyone. I want to sit here in this seat, be quiet and read my book." When a lady sat down beside me, I politely said hello to her, and she responded similarly. Nothing else was said for about 30 minutes.

Finally she disturbed my reading to inquire, "Do you think it makes any difference what religion a person belongs to?"

I almost laughed at God's sense of humor. I closed my book and replied, "Yes, I most certainly do." For the next two hours, I shared with this lady why I believe it makes an eternal difference, and she invited Jesus Christ to come into her life. Rejoicing, I disembarked from the plane a few minutes later, no longer aware of my tiredness . . .

* * *

When I became a Christian, the last thing I intended to do was to witness to someone.

I did desire to take in as much of God's Word as I could, but I was not being very honest at first. When I was at home, I lived like a Christian. But at work, I was the same old Bailey Marks. Nothing about my life would indicate to anyone that I was a Christian. I was not willing to tell anyone what had happened in my life for some months.

Then Mrs. Newbold announced to our Bible class what I thought was the worst news I had ever heard: A group of people from an organization I had never heard of called Campus Crusade for Christ was coming to Birmingham to teach us all how to share our faith. I was caught in a dilemma, because I knew if I attended a course on personal evangelism, I would no longer have a legitimate excuse not to witness. On the other hand, all our new-found Christian friends apparently were excited about this course, so it was causing a major turmoil in my life to avoid being embarrassed before them. Unknown to me, Elizabeth was going through the same trauma.

When the Campus Crusade people appeared on the scene to give their weekend training session, there was no way we could gracefully escape going on Friday night, so we went. At the conclusion of the evening, we were given an assignment to go home and write on a sheet of paper all of the sins present in our lives at that moment. My rebellious spirit countered, "Forget it." I couldn't see the point of it, and I refused to cooperate.

Very rarely did I work on Saturdays, but it's amazing how anxious I was to go to work that particular Saturday morning! Elizabeth attended the seminar all day, however, and I showed up for the evening session. Dismayed, Elizabeth greeted me with, "Do you know what we are supposed to do tomorrow? They want us to go knocking at people's homes and start talking to them about Jesus!"

I don't remember my exact comment, but I'm sure it wasn't very spiritual. I knew that Elizabeth was upset, but I didn't realize to what extent. She was literally horrified. In fact, she was so terrified that by the witnessing time the next day, she had worked herself into an emotional frenzy and was actually sick with a temperature.

As the time approached to meet at the church, she sweetly insisted that she would be all right and would just remain at home with the children, and she said that I should go on to the church and join the others. "But Elizabeth," I protested, being the good husband that I am, "the last thing I could ever do is go off and leave you at home, sick in bed, while I'm out witnessing!" So neither one of us went witnessing.

We thought we had done a masterful job of deceiving everyone. Little did we know how completely transparent we were, and how well our new Christian friends understood why

An Abundant Dimension

we had stayed home. Aware of our rebellious attitude, we were both miserable.

Elizabeth was the first to give this area to the Lord and begin to trust Him to use her. After awhile she asked a Christian friend to take her out so she could learn to share her faith in Christ. Elizabeth began to witness, and immediately others came to know Christ through her ministry, beginning with two teenage twins who were our next-door neighbors.

I was not as practical as my wife. Being the creative sort, I decided that I did not need anyone's help. I would learn to witness on my own! To say that I was obnoxious with my first attempt would be to put it mildly.

One evening while Elizabeth's brother, Wade, was visiting in our home, I began to witness to him in my own crude way. After my one-hour lecture on God, which included telling Wade what a terrible sinner he was and how much he needed God, he told me that he was not interested in anything I had said all evening. With my "gentle, loving attitude" conspicuously absent, I leaped up angrily and ordered him out of my home!

From this experience, I concluded that no one was interested in Christ, and therefore I was not going to witness anymore. Needless to say, the damage I did that night was sufficient that it took months before we could talk to Wade again about the Lord. Some months later, Wade did come to know Christ as his Savior and Lord, and today he is with the Lord, having died quite early in life. How thankful we are for that assurance that He is with Christ. We are also grateful that we didn't give up, even after that first blundering start.

Later that year, the same Campus Crusade group from Atlanta came back to conduct another Lay Institute for Evangelism in Birmingham. By that time, I was tired of being rebellious and miserable. It was a situation much like I'd experienced a year or so earlier, when I was looking for Christ: I knew that I was missing out on something important and wonderful. I could tell from the lives of other Christians around me that I was not experiencing the joyful Christian life, but I didn't understand what was wrong.

So this time, rather than scheming to find ways to miss sessions, I made sure that I was present for every one. On the second day of the training, Birmingham experienced one of the largest snowfalls it had had in decades, and attendance at the institute dropped to almost no one. But not me. I was the first one there and the last one to leave each night.

The lecturer began by describing the three types of people mentioned by the apostle Paul in I Corinthians 2:15-3:3: the natural man, the spiritual man and the carnal man. Natural man is the non-Christian — one who doesn't have Christ in his life. The spiritual man is a Christian who has Christ in his life and is allowing Christ to control his life. The carnal man is a Christian who has Christ in his life, but who refuses to allow Christ to control his life. The carnal man is in control of his own life.

As I studied these three types of people, I saw in the natural man a picture of myself for the first 31 years of my life. I also recognized my present life as that of the carnal man. As the speaker elaborated on the characteristics of the carnal man, I wondered how he knew so much about me!

According to human standards, there was no gross sin in my life, but many small areas had begun to short-circuit God's power and His freedom to use me — such things as unbelief, disobedience, a poor prayer life, worry, discouragement and a failure to share with others what God had done for me.

Then, the speaker related characteristics of the spiritual man. He is Christ-centered, is empowered by the Holy Spirit, is introducing others to Christ, has an effective prayer life, understands God's Word, trusts God, obeys God and both experiences and demonstrates the fruit of the Spirit (love, joy, peace, patience, kindness, faithfulness, goodness, gentleness, self-control).

By this time, I was sitting on the edge of my seat, saying to myself, "This is what I want. I want to be a spiritual man of God. I really want to experience the abundant life that Jesus promised to us."

But then suddenly I was confronted with the same assignment I'd rejected the year before. For the second time I was challenged to make a list of the sins in my life. This list was to be completely between God and me. I was to ask the Holy Spirit to reveal anything in my life that was not pleasing to Him and to write it on a piece of paper. Again I wrestled with my pride, realizing that until I was willing to deal with the sin in my life, there was no way I could experience the abundant life I was seeking.

But it was still a real battle of the ego to submit my will to God's will. I fought it hard that night, but I finally submitted and began making my list. I could hardly believe what was happening! As I wrote down one thing, 10 others came to my mind. I kept writing until the paper was filled on the front, the back and all of the margins!

When our lists were completed, we were asked to write across them a personalized version of I John 1:9: "If I confess my sins, God is faithful and just to forgive my sins and to cleanse me from all unrighteousness." What a relief it was to apply this promise of God to my own life! Writing out the verse, I claimed it to be true in my life and then joyfully destroyed the paper.

My sins were forgiven when I received Christ, but that evening the reality became clear to me. The Bible says, "If I regard iniquity in my heart, the Lord will not hear me" (Psalm 66:18, KJV). In other words, sin in my life broke my fellowship with God. It hindered God's freedom to work in and through me.

As I made the list of my sins that night, I realized that when I confess my sins, God places them behind His back (Isaiah 38:17), "as far as the east is from the west" (Psalm 103:12), "into the depths of the sea" (Micah 7:19) and remembers them no more (Hebrews 8:12).

This experience actually was as meaningful to me as was inviting Jesus Christ to come into my life to be my Lord and Savior. For the first time, I understood how to break the power of sin in my life, thus learning how to experience an abundant, joyful Christian life.

As the seminar went on, I discovered how I could be filled — that is, controlled by and empowered — with the Holy Spirit, by faith. The Bible says, "As you therefore have received Christ Jesus the Lord, so walk in Him" (Colossians 1:6). I had received Christ Jesus *by faith*, trusting His promise to come into my life and make me a new person. I had not expected or insisted on any special feelings. It was therefore my responsibility to also walk — live my daily life — *by faith*, trusting the Spirit of Christ to live His life through me, walking in my body, speaking with my lips, seeing with my eyes, etc.

Two verses that I didn't even know were in the Bible came to life for me that week, as they were presented in a command-promise sequence. Ephesians 5:18 commands us: "And do not get drunk with wine, for that is dissipation, but be filled with the Spirit." I John 5:14,15 gives us a promise: "And this is the confidence which we have before Him, that, if we ask anything according to His will, He hears us. And if we know that He hears us in whatever we ask, we know that we have the requests which we have asked from Him."

The command? Be filled with the Spirit.

The promise? If we ask anything according to God's will, He will grant our request. Was it God's will that I be filled with the Holy Spirit? Of course it was, for He had commanded it! Would He answer me if I asked to be filled? Yes, if I prayed according to His will. Therefore, when I asked God to fill me, and I claimed His promise that He would, I was filled, and I didn't need to expect any feelings. *I was filled by faith.*

I was liberated. I began to understand that I could live the abundant life promised to me moment by moment, day by day, week by week, by faith. I began to understand that I could walk by faith, filled with His Spirit, obeying God and allowing Him to control my life.

After learning this, I was ready to learn how to communicate my faith in Christ effectively with other people. In other words, I learned how to witness in the power of the Holy Spirit. As usually happens, it was not long before I was used by God to share the love of Christ with someone.

I was reserved and still very much afraid, so I had to be put on the spot. My pastor, the Rev. Frank Barker, came by my store one afternoon and said, "Bailey, come and go visiting for the church with me tonight." I was cornered. I had no excuse, so I went, and that was the first step.

The next step came through a very ordinary situation; I was in my office talking to a traveling furniture representative. The man had family problems, and as I listened to his troubles, the Lord kept telling me in my mind, "You have the answer to his problem." I remained silent. The man continued to talk about his problems. I continued to nod my head and remain silent. Finally, under considerable conviction that my silence was disobedience before God, I began to share with him how he could know Christ as his Savior, and my friend invited Christ to come into his life. I could hardly believe it!

This man's problems were not solved immediately, nor in exactly the way he would have liked if he'd been given the choice. But that day in my office, he had met the Problem Solver. He met the only person who promises to give us a peace that passes all understanding when we trust Him (Philippians 4:7).

Many years after leaving my business, I met my friend again, and he immediately began relating to me what Christ was doing in his life. It was thrilling to see how God had proved Himself faithful to one of the first people whom I had led to Christ.

Since that day, I've had opportunity to share Christ on a personal basis with thousands, and hundreds of them have invited Jesus Christ to come into their lives. It never gets old! Every time I see someone invite Christ into his life by faith, I taste the same joy I felt that first time in my office years ago. But I had to begin, to take a first step of faith, committing my fears and traumas to God. It meant beginning to tell my friends about Jesus, leaving the results to Him.

So many times this obedience needs to begin right in the home. When Elizabeth and I began to pray about our two children, ages five and three, we prayed that they would not wait as long as we did to become Christians. Yet we thought they were still too young to understand and accept Christ as their Savior. One day soon afterward, however, Mrs. Newbold shared with Elizabeth that one of the greatest privileges God gives to Christian parents is to help lead their own children to the Lord.

That same evening, as Elizabeth was praying with our two, Lisa (age 5) and Bailey, Jr. (age 3), she explained to Lisa how she could know Christ as her Savior. Lisa prayed and invited Jesus to come into her life. Bailey, Jr. was saying nothing, just kneeling there beside them. Elizabeth concluded that he was too young to understand.

A year later, we decided to present Bailey with an opportunity to receive Christ. Elizabeth again very carefully explained how to receive Christ and asked if he would like to do so. With a four-year-old child's simplicity, he looked up and explained to his mother, "Jesus came into my life the same night Lisa received Him." Unknown to us, the Spirit of God had been alive in this little fellow's heart for more than a year!

Today, as Christian teenagers, both of these children have confident assurance of their eternal relationship with God. It had been firmly established there on their knees beside their mother.

I have discovered that people all over the world are hungry to know God. I personally believe that millions more would come to know Christ personally every year if only Christians were mobilized, trained and obedient to communicate their faith in Christ with others.

Admittedly, it is a constant struggle for most of us to witness as a way of life. I have met few people who seem to share their faith in Christ easily. The majority are like me; it is a real struggle for me to open my mouth every time I witness.

Yet I have found that it is impossible for me to be filled with the Holy Spirit unless I am regularly communicating my faith in Christ with others. If I fail to witness, I am being disobedient, and I certainly cannot be filled with the Holy Spirit while being disobedient.

Even though I've shared Christ with thousands, each time I begin to talk to someone, the devil whispers in my ear, "He's going to think you are crazy, or even a religious fanatic . . . She'll think strange things about you if you talk about Christ . . . You'd better just keep your mouth closed." On each occasion I'm tempted to do just that, but each time that I decide instead to trust God, open my mouth and share the gospel, God blesses me almost as much as He does the individual who is hearing the gospel!

Like most people, I continually look for reasons not to witness. Thankfully, whenever I do, the Holy Spirit is faithful to nudge me gently and say, "Bailey, you are about to be disobedient." I don't want to be disobedient. I want to please the one whom I love so much. I want to respond, "Lord, I want to trust You" and to begin to talk about Him. I guess you could say that I'm compelled to share my faith — not as an obligation, but in heart appreciation for God's love for me and with an honest desire to be obedient to my Lord and Master.

I now realize that my family and I were drawn into the kingdom of God because some Christians in our community were lovingly committed to that same spirit of obedience in witnessing. When Elizabeth and I became Christians within a few months of one another in 1964, we were part of a spiritual awakening taking place in our part of town.

The two main instruments that God was using in that spiritual awakening were Elizabeth Newbold, the lady responsible for introducing both my wife and me to Christ, and the Rev. Frank Barker, pastor of Briarwood Presbyterian Church. God reached into hundreds of homes in our community through the ministry of these two people. We were privileged to meet Christ in the early stages of the awakening, and then we had opportunity to be used by the Lord in its development.

A group of young business and professional men headed by Dr. Sam Peeples, a dentist in Birmingham who had come to know Christ recently, decided to form an advisory committee for Campus Crusade for Christ in our city. All of our lives had been greatly blessed through this movement, and we desired to give leadership and financial assistance in any way we could to begin this ministry in Alabama.

Immediately, God began to bless in a powerful way. Hearts had been prepared, and we saw God's Spirit use a group of baby Christians (most of us were from 15 to 18 months old in the Lord) to help launch a campus and lay movement in Alabama that has resulted in many thousands coming to know Jesus Christ as their Savior and Lord. Theologically, we were not trained. Spiritually, we were very young. We had little experience, but God took our availability and multiplied it for His glory!

God went further to give us an international vision. A fund-raising banquet challenged us to "spiritually adopt" other countries by investing the initial funds needed to start a ministry there. As a result of this effort, Campus Crusade was established in 12 foreign countries!

None of us fully realized what was happening, but we were excited about what had occurred in our lives, and we wanted others to know Jesus Christ as we did. We were ordinary people living ordinary lives in an ordinary city — and yet because we were filled with and empowered by God's Holy Spirit, we were having an extraordinary impact upon our city and state, as well as other parts of the world.

" 'Not by might, nor by power, but by My Spirit,' says the Lord of hosts" (Zechariah 4:6). I learned in a wonderful way in those years that nothing can be accomplished in my own strength, but anything and everything can be done in the strength of the Lord.

The Holy Spirit will do His extraordinary work through me as I am available and filled with His power. What an exciting, extraordinary life!

Personal Application

Could you identify with my experience as a carnal Christian — knowing that I was missing out on the joyful, abundant Christian life but not understanding what to do about it? Then I urge you to stop right now and turn to Appendix B.

This condensed version of the message on "How to Be Filled With the Spirit" was originally given by Dr. Bill Bright, the president and founder of Campus Crusade for Christ International. It has proven extremely important in my own life and ministry.

Prayerfully evaluate your own life in the light of the Scripture and concepts shared. Be honest before God — are you experiencing a carnal life or a spiritual life? If you desire to experience a life of righteousness, joy and fruitfulness, I encourage you to pray to be filled with the Holy Spirit today.

CHAPTER THREE

Do You Want *Me*, God?

I barreled down the San Bernardino Freeway from Los Angeles International Airport, feeling extremely sorry for myself. "Is this what I left my lucrative business for?" I fumed. "Why, I could have hired someone else to do this job and stayed in business!"

Two weeks before, I had arrived with my family at Arrowhead Springs, eager to begin full-time ministry with Campus Crusade. We had no home at first, so all four of us were temporarily cramped into one room in the Arrowhead Springs Hotel. Because of the time of year at which we reported, we were given odds and ends of jobs for the first six weeks. Elizabeth babysat two very bored children, and I found myself struggling with an unchallenging job: chauffeuring people back and forth from San Bernardino to the airport!

I always spent one leg of the trip alone behind the wheel, since I was taking passengers either to or from the airport. Inevitably, I found myself arguing with the Lord each time and trying to console myself.

Driving back late that particular night, I began to sense that God was using this humbling situation to get my attention and to teach me what it means to be a servant. I recalled Jesus' words, that He "did not come to be served, but to serve" (Matthew 20:28). Christ had even washed the feet of His own disciples shortly before He went to the cross. Once again, I realized that I had to come to the point of submitting my will to the Lord.

"Okay, Lord," I sighed, "I am willing to do whatever You want me to do. I will be a chauffeur for the rest of my life if You want me to be!"

God had evidently accomplished His purpose in my life, because that night just happened to be the last time I was asked to make a chauffeur's run to the airport...

* * *

As young Christians, Elizabeth and I were involved in a

number of very fulfilling Christian activities. We traveled over the state often with a Campus Crusade training team, sharing our testimonies and helping train many people in personal evangelism. It was exciting to realize that we were actually multiplying ourselves spiritually.

At the same time, we were well off socially and financially and having loads of fun. Much of our free time and money were invested in the Lord's work, God was using us, and we were really quite satisfied.

Professionally, I was still following my boyhood ambition to be a furniture man like my Daddy. The family retail furniture business had been my life for 10 years, and I thrived on the hard work and long hours it demanded. I had always loved the challenge of building something big, making money and seeing dreams and ideas become reality. Going to work each morning meant facing a new day's challenges, and I thoroughly enjoyed it.

But one day all that began to change. I started struggling with my vocation, and my mind was not with me most of the day. It was some time before I realized that the third major struggle in my spiritual life had begun.

Not even to myself would I admit that God could possibly want me to leave my business. And yet the simple truth began to dawn on me: I really preferred to confront people with the claims of Jesus Christ rather than being confined to the administrative details of running a business. But even as I pinpointed my desire, I felt greatly obligated to my family.

At that time my father was approaching the age when he should sit back and take it easy, so I had accepted a twofold task that year: to carry a major load of the business affairs and to help train John, my younger brother who had just come into the business, to become an executive in the company. From a human perspective, I felt that I was needed very much in the business, and the other members of my family felt the same!

I began to wrestle day and night with this issue. Many of my hours driving back and forth to work that next year I spent literally arguing with the Lord. As I thought of various options, I kept saying, "No, Lord, not me. You need my money." The Lord kept saying, "No, I want you."

Aloud I would point out many sound reasons and logical

arguments why I needed to stay in Birmingham with my family. God never argued back, but I just kept hearing that still small voice saying, "Bailey, I want *you*."

It took three significant events that year to pry me away from my business and start me down a road toward the most thrilling adventure any businessman could ask for. First was a Keswick Bible Convention held in Birmingham. I'd actively participated in these Bible conferences for lay people in previous years, but I went to only one session that year. The speaker was Stuart Briscoe, and his message that morning from Acts 6 centered around the life of Stephen.

Mr. Briscoe startled me by stating that there may have been other outstanding characteristics about Stephen, but as far as we know, he was just an ordinary businessman! Evidently he was a fairly new Christian, because the church itself was young, but he was chosen along with six others to fill leadership positions. He is specifically described by God's Word as a man "full of faith and of the Holy Spirit." I was deeply impressed that his primary qualification was that he was filled with the Holy Spirit.

I walked out of the church reasoning with myself again: "You are an ordinary businessman filled with the Holy Spirit. Do you want your life to be used in the same extraordinary way Stephen's life was?" Back and forth I wavered in my struggle — desiring to be available, but for some months unwilling to trust God completely.

Finally, I was no longer filled with the Holy Spirit, nor was I experiencing the joy and peace of the Christian life. I was disobedient to God, and I would not listen to Him. For those around me, I developed my acting ability so that outwardly I was having a fine ministry. But inwardly I was rebellious and miserable.

The situation went from bad to worse, and in October I reached the end of my rope. The second significant event occurred as I was scheduled to leave town with my brother, John, on a major buying trip. At that point I was an emotional wreck. I knew I was in no frame of mind to spend large sums of the company's money and work with John on his first buying expedition.

So I got on the telephone to the only two individuals I had ever sought spiritual counsel from: Mrs. Elizabeth Newbold and the Rev. Frank Barker. Through the first call I discovered that one of Frank's children was very ill, and he and his wife had been at the hospital with the child all day. I learned on the second call that Mrs. Newbold was out of the city!

I sat down to dinner that evening and told my wife, "I cannot go on the buying trip tomorrow unless a radical change takes place in my life tonight." Distraught, I finally got up from the dinner table and telephoned Frank at the hospital. I asked him to stop by on his way home that evening, regardless of the time — I would be waiting up for him.

According to my calculation, our home was a 15-minute drive from the hospital, but 10 minutes later, Frank was at our door. Apparently the Spirit of God convinced him that I needed help!

For the first time to someone other than Elizabeth, I poured out my dilemma. "Most of this year," I explained, "I have felt that God is asking me to leave my business. But, in my opinion, God does not understand my situation. I can't leave!"

Frank's reply was pointed: "Bailey, does God own every area of your life?" I immediately replied, "Yes, Frank, He does!"

Logically, Frank must have thought, "Now if God does control every area of Bailey's life, why did he just tell me that he wants control so far as his business is concerned?" Wisely, he overlooked the obvious contradiction and said, "Bailey, let's take spiritual inventory." That seemed appropriate to me, so he went down the list.

Frank asked if I had given my wife to God. I answered, "Yes, I have given Elizabeth to Him."

"Does God own your children? Your finances? Your social position? Your ability to make money?" We continued down the long list, as I repeated, "Yes, God owns that . . . Yes, I have given that to Him also." Everything had been surrendered.

Then Frank looked at me and stated quietly, "Bailey, you've told me that God owns your finances and also your ability to make money. Have you turned over to the Lord what you consider the need for your physical presence in the family business?"

It hurt to admit it, but he was on target. "No, Frank, I haven't."

He kindly exhorted me, "Well, then, you haven't committed 100% of your life to the Lord, have you?"

I had to be honest with myself, honest with Frank and most important, honest with the Lord. "No, I haven't." Slowly it began to sink in that God was asking for my willingness, my availability — the same things Stephen had given to the Lord. As Frank went on to explain, God might want me to leave the business, or possibly He might even want me to remain in Birmingham in the furniture business for the rest of my life. Whatever the case, the question was my availability, my willingness to do anything He wanted me to do.

Again Frank asked a pointed question: "Bailey, are you willing to do that?"

I didn't have to consider very long until my answer came: "Yes, I am." Kneeling beside my chair, I prayed a prayer of surrender. "Lord, I am willing to do whatever You want me to do with my life. If You want me to stay here in Birmingham, I am willing to stay here. Or if You want me to go off to some deep, dark river in the middle of the jungle with all the snakes and crocodiles, then I am willing to do that, too."

An amazing thing happened to me while on my knees that night. I felt God blanketing me with His love, as if He placed His arms around me to say, "Bailey, this is all I want from you."

A few minutes earlier I'd been an emotional wreck, but I stood to my feet a changed man. I was experiencing that peace which passes all understanding, promised by Jesus Himself: "Peace I leave with you; My peace I give to you; not as the world gives, do I give to you. Let not your heart be troubled, nor let it be fearful" (John 14:27).

In less than 45 minutes, Frank was on his way back to the hospital, and when Elizabeth returned home with the children soon afterward, her first words were, "What happened to you?" Before I could answer, she continued. "When I left, you were like a caged lion! Now you seem to be a different man. You're so calm."

The difference was a simple "yes" to the Lord, which had ended my year-long struggle. I'd given the reins to God, assured that because He was in control, He would show me what He wanted me to do. In return, I was transformed by His peace. The next morning, in an entirely new mental attitude, I left with John on our trip.

Over the next three months, Elizabeth and I talked at length about the direction our lives were taking. Did the Lord want us to leave the business? That question was always before us, but now our attitude was one of willingness and peace. We were frightened at the thought of leaving, but also full of excited suspense.

I was fascinated by the freedom from anxiety we enjoyed during those months of uncertainty. We continued our normal activities on a day-to-day basis, no longer overly concerned about the situation, and I probably was more effective in my business during that period than I had been for many months.

The third and final event which pried me loose from my business occurred on January 14, 1967. It began like many other Saturday mornings. Elizabeth was preparing breakfast, and I was in our bedroom reading from *My Utmost for His Highest,* a devotional book by Oswald Chambers. Commenting on Isaiah 6:8, Mr. Chambers observed:

> CALLED OF GOD. "Whom shall I send, and who will go for us? Then said I, Here am I; send me." Isaiah 6:8.
>
> God did not address the call to Isaiah; Isaiah overheard God saying, "Who will go for us?" The call of God is not for the special few, it is for everyone. Whether or not I hear God's call depends upon the state of my ears; and what I hear depends upon my disposition. "Many are called but few are chosen," that is, few prove themselves the chosen ones. The chosen ones are those who have come into a relationship with God through Jesus Christ whereby their disposition has been altered and their ears unstopped, and they hear the still small voice questioning all the time, "Who will go for us?" It is not a question of God singling out a man and saying, "Now, you go." God did not lay a strong compulsion on Isaiah; Isaiah was in the presence of God and he overheard the call, and realized that there was nothing else for him but to say, in conscious freedom, "Here am I, send me." Get out of your mind the idea of expecting God to come with compulsions and pleadings. When our Lord called His disciples there was no irresistible compulsion from outside. The quiet passionate insistence of His "Follow Me" was spoken to men with every power wide awake. If we let the Spirit of God bring us face to face with God, we too shall hear something akin to what Isaiah heard, the still small voice of God, and in perfect freedom will say, "Here am I; send me."[1]

I was intrigued by Mr. Chambers' point that God was not speaking directly to Isaiah. God was talking aloud, and Isaiah's attention was so focused on God that he overheard Him saying, "Whom shall I send?"

Isaiah's natural response, because of His relationship with the Lord, was: "Here am I, send me."

Rising from the edge of the bed, I went to the kitchen, took the frying pan off the stove and asked Elizabeth to read that portion about Isaiah. When she finished, we both looked at each other and agreed that God was speaking to us, saying, "Whom shall I send?" Right there in the kitchen, we obediently said, "Lord, here we are; send us."

This was the most difficult thing I had ever done. Yet, I knew that this was what God wanted, and I wanted to be in the perfect center of His will for my life.

Where do you begin when you feel God wants you to "start over"? Leaving your business and entering some area of Christian ministry is a mammoth decision. We prayed, "Lord, what is Your perfect will for us?"

We contemplated seminary, but quickly ruled it out. I was 34 and didn't want to return to the books. Also, the impression of Stephen, an ordinary businessman, was still in my mind. Stephen was not theologically trained. During my first three years as a Christian, I had studied the Bible regularly and had gone to every Bible class that my schedule would allow. I felt I should continue in that fashion to increase my knowledge of God's Word, trusting God to use me as he had Stephen.

We considered several other possibilities, but as I prayed about the Christian organizations and opportunities for a person of my experience, there was only one place where we sensed He was leading us. Campus Crusade for Christ had had a major influence on us as we were growing in the Lord, and we had been deeply involved in its ministry. I personally knew of no other organization at that time in which I could be used by God in such an effective way. Elizabeth and I concluded that this was where God was sending us, and we immediately submitted our application to join the staff of Campus Crusade.

Then came the difficult part. In fairness to my parents and brothers, I knew I must share our intentions with them even before we were accepted on the staff. It came as a hard surprise to all of them. All of the reasons I'd given to the Lord in the preceding months were also raised by my family to persuade me to remain in the business! There were sad and tense moments, and even a few angry ones.

But even though I could not come up with a logical explanation to cause our families to understand and accept this decision, God used this difficulty to confirm His call to us. We had to leave the circumstances in His hands, and only through the years has the miracle He performed become apparent. For one thing, I was never missed in the business — it grew faster without me than it had with me! And in addition, as the years passed, all of our families eventually accepted what we were doing as God's will for us.

A few weeks after our announcement to the family, we were accepted on the staff of Campus Crusade. Then came another real faith-stretcher! We had to sell our beautiful home, tidy up our affairs and raise our own personal support.

Elizabeth and I had talked about raising our financial support, and we had agreed that we were willing to do that. However, it was one of those faraway dreams that becomes another story when you wake up one morning and realize the dream is real. I was supposed to go and ask people to support me financially! An indignant thought pattern began: "I've never had to ask or beg for a thing in my life. But now that I've given my life to Christ to serve Him, this is the reward I get?"

Immediately, I recognized this was unbelief, and I confessed my negative attitude. Then, it occurred to me that those staff members we had invested in during the previous years had never looked like beggars to us! The truth was, we had been excited about the opportunity to invest in their ministries.

Once again, God proved His faithfulness, and our total support was raised within a few days. In fact, only two of the people I contacted did not invest in our ministry!

Then the unexpected happened. It was time to sell our beautiful home overlooking the golf course. We had discussed this many times, and both of us knew it was part of His plan. However, for Elizabeth, this had been merely a future dream — just as support-raising had been for me. The stark reality of what we were doing suddenly hit her, and she fell apart on me, went to bed and refused to show the house to interested

Do You Want Me, *God?*

buyers. Only a few days passed until she recognized her unbelief, confessed her defeated attitude and bounded back with great enthusiasm. Within a week we had graciously turned over our home to the new owners, my brother and his family, and we were on our way to Arrowhead Springs, the international headquarters of Campus Crusade for Christ in San Bernardino, Calif.

Little did I know the growing pains we were all about to experience as we settled into a new way of life. Growing up spiritually was tough for me, probably because the Lord had quite a time getting my attention.

I was to learn, beginning with the chauffeuring lesson, that God wanted me, all right, but He wanted me as a servant. Time and again I've found myself in situations where I have reviewed that conversation with the Lord late one night on the San Bernardino Freeway:

"Do you want *me,* Lord?"

"Yes, I want *you,* Bailey — not your service, or your money, or your talent and ability. I want *you,* an ordinary businessman, to be clay in My hands, so that I can shape and mold you in any way I see fit.

"Be another Stephen, Bailey — available to do whatever I ask, willing to trust Me always."

Personal Application

The night I totally surrendered my life to Christ is burned indelibly in my mind. I have since been confronted with many similar situations, and each time I have discovered that God asks me to be available and willing to trust Him *before* He reveals His plan to me. He wants 100% of my life, nothing less.

Are you wrestling with the Lord as I did a number of years ago? I encourage you to take spiritual inventory, just as I did with Frank Barker. Determine if there is any unsurrendered area of your life, and commit it to God.

I can give you no better advice than Frank gave me the night I totally committed myself to Christ: Maybe God wants you to stay right where you are, and maybe He wants you to get up and go somewhere else. In either case, your responsibility is to be available. He will be faithful to reveal to you His perfect will. And meanwhile, He'll flood you with the peace that passes all understanding!

---

1. Oswald Chambers, *My Utmost for His Highest* (New York: Dodd, Mead & Company, 1935), p. 14.

CHAPTER FOUR

The Most Extraordinary Businessman I Know

It was probably the most shocking experience of my short Christian life.

I had been serving the Lord only a few months with Campus Crusade when I witnessed a crisis in our ministry. A group of individuals came to Dr. Bill Bright, the president and founder of our movement, with some very heated accusations. Their words were strong and demanding, and I could hardly believe what I was hearing.

In shock, I agonized, "Lord, why are You allowing me to be involved in this unhappy situation?"

Within a matter of minutes, I began to realize why I was there. I was about to witness a supernatural response to one of the most difficult situations I have ever seen a man experience . . .

* * *

I was visiting Tehran, Iran, a number of years ago when I was first asked the question which I now hear frequently: "Mr. Marks, why do you feel that God is blessing the ministry of Campus Crusade in such a significant way all over the world!"

I was humbled by the question, and the answer did not come quickly. My heart rose up in thankfulness to God for the opportunity to be part of a ministry such as this, but I weighed my words carefully.

"This ministry is the Lord's ministry, so any credit and glory belongs to the Lord Himself. Perhaps I can single out four major reasons why I believe God is blessing this ministry:

1. A strong emphasis is placed on the lordship of Jesus Christ.
2. The ministry of the Holy Spirit is thoroughly and practically taught.
3. A healthy emphasis on aggressive evangelism is upheld constantly.

4. God singled out and imparted the vision of this movement to a man whom He knew He could trust."

That man is the founder and president of Campus Crusade, Dr. Bill Bright ... the most extraordinary businessman I have ever met.

Dr. Bright's personal emphasis on the lordship of Christ, his teaching on the ministry of the Holy Spirit and his own consistent ministry of aggressive evangelism have made these items the backbone of this movement.

I believe that all the definitions of leadership that I've ever heard could be summed up in the man God called to establish and direct our ministry. But to me, the most important characteristic of his fine leadership is Bill Bright's walk with the Lord.

I first met Dr. Bright after a luncheon in Birmingham, when I was still in the furniture business. I approached him to introduce myself and thank him for his message. I still remember his very first words to me: "Mr. Marks, have you ever made the wonderful discovery of knowing Jesus Christ as your Savior and Lord?" I assured him that I had, and we proceeded with our conversation.

I remember that occasion for two very distinct reasons: First, this encounter typifies Dr. Bright's life-style. Wherever he is, whomever he meets — he always confronts people with the person of Jesus Christ. Second, apart from my wife and mother, Bill Bright was (and still is) the only person in my life who has ever tried to witness to me! His consistency in asking me that vital question is an unforgettable reminder of the urgency with which I must pursue the same life-style of directly confronting others with the gospel.

My second encounter with Dr. Bright occurred one Sunday morning after Elizabeth and I had been on staff for six weeks. We were leaving a church service when Bill and his wife, Vonette, invited us to join them for lunch. During the course of the meal, Bill shared with us his need for a personal assistant.

Two things he said impressed me. First, he explained he was looking for a man who really wanted his life to count for the Lord. Second, he needed a person who liked hard work.

I remember thinking, "I am used to hard work." But even more, I wanted my life to count for the Lord. Before I knew it, I heard words coming out of my mouth: "I would like to be the man to assist you."

Although I was completely an unknown factor to Dr. Bright, two days later he telephoned to ask if I was serious about wanting to become his assistant. I replied, "Yes, I am."

Once again he spelled out how difficult the job would be. It would require a lot of traveling and many long hours away from my family. "But if you are still interested," he continued, "I would like for you to become my personal assistant."

Thus began the fabulous year-and-a-half appointment which was such a vital part of my personal spiritual growth. During those 18 months, I had opportunity to observe Dr. Bright's actions and attitudes in every type of situation imaginable. His consistent responses to the unexpected set an excellent example for me, and only God knows how often I rely on the lessons I learned during those months. Bill Bright remains to me a living example of the Spirit-filled life.

Occasionally people ask me, "What is the greatest lesson that you learned from Bill Bright while serving as his assistant?" My reply always has a double answer: First, Bill Bright is a man of faith, and that faith is contagious! Learning more about trusting God and believing Him to do the impossible is what I "caught" from Bill Bright. Second, Bill's ability to rejoice in all situations has ministered to me at a very deep level.

I once read a very extensive interview conducted with Dr. Bright by a Christian magazine reporter. The interviewer seemed to think Bill Bright was some kind of fake, because he never appears to have any problems.

I can verify that because Dr. Bright directs a worldwide ministry with a staff of more than 11,000, he has more problems than one can possibly imagine. However, he knows the Problem Solver, and he has learned the secret of dealing with any problem in a split second. He immediately casts his cares on the Lord (according to I Peter 5:7), rejoices always (according to I Thessalonians 5:18), and as a result, he experiences the peace that passes all understanding (Philippians 4:4-7).

When Dr. Bright was confronted with the sad situation mentioned at the beginning of this chapter, I stood by stunned. My turmoil deepened as he listened quietly to his accusers, and I thought, "His heart must be broken."

Enduring the extreme verbal abuse, Dr. Bright never once tried to retaliate. When they had all left, he asked me to kneel with him, and he began to pray. Immediately, he began to rejoice over the tragic situation that had just occurred!

Astonished, I looked at him to make sure that the man I was praying with was real! Dr. Bright continued to tell the Lord that he did not understand the situation, nor was it for him to understand. He asked God to teach him everything He wanted him to learn from this experience, and he even thanked God for the various accusations which had been hurled at him.

Although he was deeply hurt, Dr. Bright never stopped rejoicing. He knew the secret of abiding in the Lord Jesus, and he responded as he knew God had commanded him to respond — by demonstrating a thankful, trusting spirit.

I have no idea what might have happened to weaken and disrupt this movement had Dr. Bright resorted to not trusting God at that time. But because he was operating as a Spirit-filled Christian, our ministry was instead strengthened. In fact, a record number of new staff joined the movement the next year, and our ministry saw an unusual harvest of souls. At the very height of the crisis, which continued over the next several months, God gave Dr. Bright the dynamic concept on how to love by faith — a concept which has helped change the lives of hundreds of thousands of Christians! And all because one man was committed, with every fiber of his being, to an extraordinary life-style.

My "training program" during those 18 months was intense. The testings that God allowed me to participate in along with Bill Bright were numerous and varied. But they were all in preparation for an adventure which was ahead of me. What a privilege has been mine to have a leader set such an example for me.

After 28 years of giving leadership to the worldwide ministry of Campus Crusade, this extraordinary businessman, Bill Bright, is still faced with phenomenal problems . . . and is still rejoicing!

Personal Application

Are you tense or "uptight" about any difficulty in your own life and ministry at this point? I have found, through Dr.

The Most Extraordinary Businessman I Know

Bright's example and my own experience, that at the very moment I am able to take my eyes off the circumstances and turn them to the Lord Jesus — meditating upon His promises and rejoicing in the situation — God immediately and supernaturally raises me above the situation. The peace that He promises becomes mine! The secret is to rejoice by thanking and praising God.

I challenge you, no matter what problem faces you at this moment, to stop right now and rejoice over the difficulty. The Scriptures admonish you to do so before the circumstances control you and short-circuit your faith. No matter what seems to be happening to you, God's supernatural peace is waiting for you. Let me repeat the apostle Paul's great admonition, from Philippians 4:4-7:

> "Rejoice in the Lord always; again I will say, rejoice! Let your forbearing spirit be known to all men. The Lord is near. Be anxious for nothing, but in everything, by prayer and supplication with thanksgiving, let your requests be made known to God. And the peace of God, which surpasses all comprehension, shall guard your hearts and your minds in Christ Jesus."

CHAPTER FIVE

Check-out for Asia

The local internists and surgeons were baffled. I was a beautiful shade of yellow, and very ill . . . and yet I had remained on my feet in a demanding travel schedule for nearly six weeks!

My illness began on my first visit to Asia after being appointed director of affairs of that area, a two-month swing through 11 nations of the Orient and Middle East. Graciously — and miraculously — God had supplied the strength for me to get out of bed each day and keep going, and through the whole trip I missed only one appointment.

But soon after my return I found myself flat on my back in a California hospital, where I lay for a full month with no idea what my illness was. I had terrible nightmares, and my mind circled endlessly around an unspoken fear: "If I ever get out of this hospital, I'll have to travel to Asia again and will probably die in an Asian hospital someday!"

The Lord taught me a number of crucial lessons while He had my complete attention there in that hospital room. Most important, I discovered that commitment to God is not a once-in-a-lifetime experience. It requires a continual application of faith. In fact, this testing experience and two others were used by God to confirm and seal my call to Asia . . .

* * *

One hot afternoon late in the summer of 1968, I sat in Dr. Bright's office going over some business with him. I had been his personal assistant for almost one and a half years, and I liked my job.

Suddenly, Dr. Bright looked at me and said, "I want you to become the Asian director." As he proceeded to challenge me, my mind immediately reviewed my lack of qualifications and why I should not assume such a position. I began to explain these reasons to Dr. Bright. In so many words, I told him that he must be out of his mind to suggest such a thing.

He replied, "I have been praying about it, and I think you are the man God would have fulfill that responsibility." He then asked me to pray about it and let him know my answer in the morning.

Elizabeth's first words, when I walked in the kitchen that evening and reported the challenge Dr. Bright had given to me, were, "You're crazy!"

I responded, "Yes, that is what I told Bill."

Later that night, I sat alone and asked God to reveal to me what He wanted me to do. I began to search the Scriptures for the answer.

I began with the many verses relating to the Great Commission and the fact that men are lost without Christ. But I continued to search for something more dramatic. Maybe I was expecting to open my Bible and spot a verse which read, "Go to Asia." My search for a dramatic experience was so intense that I was just about to close my eyes, flip the page of my Bible and place my finger to see where it would land.

Then I recalled a similar night, when on my knees with Pastor Frank Barker I had told God I was available and ready to go or to stay. I realized this new decision was simply an extension of that initial commitment. So once again, I told God I was willing to do anything He wanted me to do, and I was trusting Him to reveal His will to me. At peace, I put up my Bible and went to bed without any anxiety whatever over the monumental decision I must make in a few hours.

The next morning as I awoke, I experienced one of those unusual times when God gave me an immediate answer in a special way. There was simply no question in my mind. I knew that God wanted us to go to Asia.

As I rolled over, those were my first words to Elizabeth, and she replied, "The Lord is saying the same thing to me."

Today it frightens me to look back and realize how little I knew about Asia when I accepted this position. I did have two things going for me: an intense desire to be used by God and an ability to get things organized.

Several days later, Dr. Bright officially gave me this responsibility, with the title of director of affairs of the Asia-South Pacific ministry. Within weeks, I was off on an extensive two-month trip across Asia to become acquainted with our directors and staff in each Asian country where we had a ministry.

The Lord had some surprises in store for me. For one thing,

my reception in many countries was far from what I had anticipated. I discovered that it would take some time for our Asian staff to learn to know me and accept my style of leadership. And on the other hand, I had a lot to learn about Asian thought patterns and how to communicate through cultural differences. I can now look back at some of those first experiences and laugh, but they were not humorous at the time.

Also, I quickly observed a critical need for more continuity of our ministry from country to country. We needed to develop a more systematic, efficient movement of aggressive evangelism and discipleship across Asia if we were serious about seeing the Great Commission fulfilled on that vast continent. This required changes, which are never easy.

But through all this, I was soon to see our hearts bound together, uniting a fantastic team of men and women of many nationalities. This team continued to form as God strengthened some, removed others and raised up new leadership. As a result, I soon saw a group of men and women working together in almost every country of the Orient and South Pacific, their one common goal to glorify the Lord Jesus Christ in helping to fulfill the Great Commission in Asia in our generation.

But halfway through this initial trip, I became very ill. As I have already related, medical science could not account for the fact that although I was desperately ill, I had remained on my feet for weeks! God had truly performed a miracle and enabled me to continue my schedule despite my sickness.

Finally, after two weeks of countless tests, my doctors decided to perform exploratory surgery. They discovered that my liver had almost completely stopped functioning! But after a month of hospitalization and three months of limited activity during recuperation, I was traveling once again. Today, I live with what is called a crippled liver, but with supplementary vitamins and health foods I have no problems.

Once I was back on my feet again, it became very obvious to Elizabeth and me that it was impractical to live in California and direct a ministry in Asia! We began praying about moving our family once again — this time 9,000 miles to Asia.

After completing a very long, detailed list on all the reasons we should relocate in Singapore, I went to discuss it with Dr. Bright one September afternoon. As I presented him with the list, he asked, "What is this?"

When he learned what it was, he never even read the list. He simply inquired, "When do you want to move?" He approved our plan to leave California around the first of December, 1969, and the schedule was set for launching out into the most exciting years of my life.

The next month, October, was consumed with another trip to the Orient, and then we had 45 days to sell our home in San Bernardino, close all of our affairs, raise additional support for travel and shipping expenses, pack a container and depart from the United States. Once again we saw the Lord do that which we could never have done in our own strength, and we left on schedule the last day of November.

Enroute to our new home in Singapore, we were able to combine some family time with ministry activities in the Middle East. Consequently, we were privileged to spend the Christmas season in the Holy Land, and from there we flew to Lebanon to join our staff there.

It was the first of two experiences on our way to Asia to make a lasting impact on our family. When we arrived in Beirut, Lebanon, we were surprised to find no one at the airport to greet us. Our coming had been delayed nearly 24 hours, but we had sent cables well in advance, so we assumed they knew of our schedule change. However, no one was there.

Not overly concerned, I snapped open my briefcase and reached for my address list. Surprise: only a post office box was listed for our Lebanese director! "Oh well," I thought, "I will simply telephone him." Searching through the Beirut telephone directory, I found that neither the name of our director nor our ministry could be found in its pages.

Secretly a bit alarmed, I insisted to my family that there was no problem. "I was in Beirut last year," I reminded them. "I can take you right to the home of our director without any difficulty."

Confidently, we climbed into a taxi and proceeded to drive to the Ras Beirut area of the city. We rode up and down the streets again and again. All of the buildings looked exactly alike! I was out of ideas, so we checked into a hotel.

As we settled into our rooms, I suggested that we stop to thank the Lord for the situation. So we prayed and told the Lord that we did not understand the situation. Nonetheless, we thanked Him, as He told us to do in I Thessalonians 5:18.

Check-out for Asia

Lisa and Bailey were nine and eight years old at the time, and they probably thought it was strange to thank God for our problem, but they thanked Him right along with Elizabeth and me.

Then it seemed logical for me to go back out on the street, get my bearings straight and try to find our director's apartment. So I asked the family to wait and started to the door. But they did not want to be left behind so all four of us went down in the elevator.

It could not have been more than five minutes after we had thanked the Lord for what He was going to do in this situation when we walked out of the hotel and my eyes rested on Adel Masri, the national director of Lebanon Campus Crusade for Christ! Our eyes made contact at the same time, and suddenly my Arab brother and I were laughing and embracing each other there on the street. Our two children looked on in total amazement.

Adel explained that he was just returning from the post office with the cable and letter we had sent in his hand. They had been delayed for one week, so he had just discovered that our family must be somewhere in Beirut. At the same time we had been thanking the Lord in our hotel room, he was walking home from the post office, also giving thanks to God for the situation and wondering how to find us!

A coincidence? Rather, God's sovereign way of honoring the faith of His children. If we had not paused to pray, we would have missed Adel. God graciously arranged Adel's steps to pass the hotel at the moment we walked out the door.

Several days later we arrived in our new home town, Singapore. Again God had a special experience in store which would greatly influence our lives.

Thrilled to be there at last, we unloaded all of our luggage from the taxi and went to check into the hotel where we would spend our first night as a family in Southeast Asia. But in the excitement and confusion, I left my briefcase in the taxi.

Now, taxi drivers in large cities are not noted for their honesty, and the desk clerk in our hotel was not very encouraging. He candidly remarked, "Sir, you probably will never see your briefcase again." But our passports, visa authorizations, money, letters of credit and many other valuable items were in that briefcase!

Entering our room, we told the Lord once again that we did not understand why this had happened. But we thanked Him for the situation, and we also thanked Him that the briefcase would be returned to us that evening.

Later that evening, a telephone call came from the airport stating that my briefcase had been returned! When our driver opened his trunk back at the airport for another passenger's luggage, he discovered my briefcase. Our prayers were answered abundantly when he promptly took it to the airport officials, asking them to return it to us at the hotel where he had taken us.

I would not trade these two very dramatic lessons in faith for anything. Not only were they great learning experiences for Elizabeth and me, but the lessons also were invaluable for Lisa and Bailey. They learned right then to thank the Lord no matter what the circumstances might be. Since then, they have personally had many opportunities to say "Thank You, Lord" in some very difficult situations.

One such occasion was a personal family crisis which we faced about one year later. Our third child, Rebecca, was only a few months old when we discovered that she had contacted dengue fever. She was hospitalized in serious condition for several days, during which time Elizabeth stayed in the hospital with her. One night after our hospital visit, Lisa and Bailey, Jr. and I went out and climbed into the car to return home. All three of us were crying, shaken to see how sick their baby sister really was. But before I could say anything to comfort my children, Lisa looked up at me and said, "Daddy, let's thank the Lord that Becca is so sick!"

That evening I realized that practicing the principle of thanksgiving by faith had charted a new way of life for us as a family! Truly, answering God's call to Asia has been the adventure of our lives, as He has taken us from one faith-building incident to the next.

Personal Application

Almost every time I have made a fresh commitment to God or extended my ministry into a new involvement, a time of testing has followed. My first response as a Christian was to blame my troubles on Satan, but I believe that gives the devil more credit than he is due. In fact, the Lord usually leads us into an area of testing to be sure we really mean business for Him.

Take the life of our Lord for an example. Immediately following His baptism, Jesus was led into the wilderness and tested. Now it was the devil who tempted Him after 40 days and nights of fasting. But who led Jesus into the wilderness? The Spirit!

Perhaps you have made a specific, honest commitment in some area, and to your surprise, everything seems to be going wrong ever since! It may be a difficult situation — the loss of a loved one, a disappointment — but whatever the details, you are finding it hard to obey I Thessalonians 5:18, "In everything give thanks."

Let me assure you that saying "Thank You" to God does not require that you be in an emotionally happy frame of mind. However, it does mean that you acknowledge our sovereign God's absolute control. He loves you very much, and when you are filled with the Holy Spirit, He will see that every situation works for your good.

If recent tests of your commitment to God have discouraged or confused you, I urge you to read once again Romans 8:28, and then say, as an act of your will, "Thank You, God." With those three words, He shifts the burden from your shoulders to His own.

CHAPTER SIX

Multiply and Conquer

We were enjoying a cup of tea together during a management training conference in Madras when the Indian pastor shared his story with me.

In the past year, he had observed a vital spiritual explosion on a nearby university campus. So he invited one of our campus staff members to conduct a Lay Institute for Evangelism (LIFE) in his church. Once his congregation had taken the same training in evangelism and discipleship being given to the Christian students, their attendance increased rapidly from approximately 75 to 200.

"But, Mr. Marks," he insisted, "the major blessing has been in my own life!" He went on to tell me that during his 20 years of pastoral ministry before this LIFE, he had never led anyone to Christ. However, through the training and the personal interest of this young staff member, God changed his life, and he began to witness.

He concluded by saying, "Since I led my first soul to the Lord, I have had the privilege of introducing at least one person to the Lord every day. Nine months have gone by, and God has used me to lead more than 300 people to Christ!"

You can imagine how elated I was. I had the distinct impression that this gentleman shared Christ with enthusiasm wherever he went! But I was sobered once again by the reminder that training can make such a strategic difference in the life of an individual Christian . . .

* * *

When I began ministering in Asia in 1968, I found our ministry there going in many different directions. Throughout Asia and the South Pacific, Campus Crusade was being directed by men of God who desired to serve the Lord and see their countries reached for Christ. But we lacked a real cutting edge. Many people were busy doing a variety of things — most of them "good things," but not always the things which fit together toward our overall goal.

Campus Crusade works as a unit with other evangelical organizations and denominations in our goal: the fulfillment of our Lord's Great Commission throughout the world. But we are differentiated by the ways and methods we employ to reach this goal. There are many great Christian organizations, missions and denominations working across the Orient which have been involved in helping to expose Asia to the gospel for scores of years. The thousands of churches and millions of Christians across Asia attest to God's blessing upon their ministries. But it was my desire that our movement believe God for even more extraordinary things.

As I evaluated the situation in our Asian ministry, I realized the problem: We had no clear-cut strategy which would enable us to perpetuate the philosophy of our movement. We all agreed that our philosophy was threefold — win men and women to Christ, build them in their faith and send them to reach the world — but just how we were to implement this was not always clearly defined in each country's ministry.

I began to pray that God would use Campus Crusade in every country in the Orient as a vital force to help unite the churches and to direct our efforts toward the fulfillment of the Great Commission. I prayed that the vision which God had given Dr. Bright many years ago, along with the prayer target for the fulfillment of the vision by 1980, would become a reality in every Asian country. This was not a selfish prayer to see our movement become bigger and better known than others, but it came from my honest desire to see our movement used mightily by the Lord in helping to reach Asians with His love and forgiveness.

I prayed that God would allow us to form and shape a movement of such significant impact that it would be worthy of the respect of church leaders across Asia and the South Pacific. With all my heart, I prayed for such supernatural results through our ministry that it would be undeniable that this was a work not of men but of God — and therefore He would receive *all* the glory.

But how? How was the philosophy of winning, building and sending people for Christ to start happening on a large scale all across Asia?

God singled out His man, Kent Hutcheson, to assist me in

a tangible answer to this question. Kent and his wife, Diane, had been ministering in Southeast Asia for several years, having had outstanding ministries of spiritual multiplication in the United States for a number of years. When they moved to Singapore in 1968, Kent was to play a major role in developing and building the Asian ministry. Kent has defined terms, developed curriculum, established strategies and led training programs until today a movement of spiritual multiplication literally is sweeping across the Asian continent.

Kent and I became as close as brothers, praying, witnessing, traveling and living near each other. Our conversations always turned to the question, "What will it take to turn Campus Crusade in Asia into a movement characterized by radical spiritual multiplication?"

Webster's dictionary defined a movement for us: "A series of organized activities by people working concertedly toward some goal; the organization consisting of those activities." In other words, a movement involves people who are working together to accomplish a goal.

In order to define our goals, Kent eventually refined and put together our own definition of what we desired to see accomplished: "A movement is a group of people embracing a common purpose and philosophy who are moving toward defined goals and objectives and who are committed to the spreading and the multiplication of those goals and objectives through the constant repetition and propagation of their belief."

It followed logically, we concluded, that there was no way possible to build this type of movement without careful, uniform training in spiritual multiplication. Training makes the difference. An excellent education and theological degrees do not necessarily train a person to be a spiritual multiplier.

We considered the excellent materials already available and in use in our ministry worldwide, and we set about to develop a curriculum that would maximize their use in training others. At the same time, both of us saw an increasing need to designate a central location for the training of our leaders and new staff. It was nearly four years later, in February of 1972, that our dreams became a reality and the Great Commission Training Center was established in Manila, Philippines, under Kent's direction. At last we had a center to train our staff to become spiritual multipliers, to insure the continuity the Asian ministry so desperately needed.

Kent was not content for our training center to become an institution in which knowledge was simply transferred. He specified that each staff member in training should spend approximately one-third of his time in theoretical classroom training and two-thirds of his time in practical training on the field. For example, on one morning a trainee would study some guidelines to help turn a conversation to spiritual matters in order to share the gospel. In the afternoon, he would practice these guidelines in real situations, trusting the Holy Spirit not only to develop in him the skill desired but also to reach people in the process.

The trainee would be considered trained when both he and his trainer were assured that he could return to his home country and develop a ministry of spiritual multiplication. He would need to possess adequate biblical knowledge as well as the "how to's" of winning, building and sending other individuals in his own culture. The training process would require a detailed array of "check-out" procedures through which the trainee would demonstrate his grasp of both theory and practice.

The first session, enrolling staff from Indonesia, the Philippines and Japan, was conducted in the Hutchesons' home in Manila. Now the six-month training sessions average from 40 to 50 staff members from as many as 12 different Oriental cultures in training together. The Manila base continues to serve as a model for Asia, with five additional training centers established in the Orient and several more to open soon.

With the continent of Asia leading the way for our worldwide ministry in establishing the concepts of a uniform curriculum and a central training location, training centers have since been established in Africa, Latin America, the Middle East, Europe and North America. Kent Hutcheson has returned to the United States to develop and direct the entire international training curriculum program.

The present director of the Manila base, Henry Tan, came through the training center himself several years ago. A Malaysian of Chinese descent, Henry has a master's degree in business management, and his wife, Wilma, is a Filipina. Included on his staff of senior trainers are Nils and Sandy Becker, who have served in Asia for 12 years, mostly with Korea Campus Crusade.

Although it took time for us to see the effect of the training center concept on our ministry, there were clear signs that our movement was growing and gaining momentum through this strong training emphasis. Dramatic evidences of proper training began to be noticed in a number of countries.

Our ministry in Taiwan (Republic of China) is a good example. In 1974, our ministry there was still primarily a campus outreach, and we were not having the impact upon the whole society for which we had been praying. After a thorough evaluation, all of us agreed: The majority of the Chinese staff were not adequately trained to do the job necessary.

Although it was a difficult decision, the director, Jonathan Chiu, chose to close the ministry in two cities in order to bring his entire staff into the newly-established Great Commission Training Center at Taichung for six months.

There was an immediate testing of his decision, as some of the staff were unhappy over it. We loved these brothers and sisters, and we did not want to lose any from our staff over this difficult move; but we knew we must stand fast in faithfulness to do that which we believed God had called us to do.

God immediately honored the faith of Jonathan and the others, for no one resigned from staff, except one for another reason. And during the first month of the Taichung training center's operation, more people were exposed to the gospel through our Taiwan staff than had heard the claims of Christ over the past entire year!

That was only the beginning. As our staff members faithfully involved themselves in a ministry of spiritual multiplication on campuses and in their communities, pastors all over Taiwan began to realize that if their congregations were trained in the same way, great things would start happening in and through their churches.

The stage was set, and by the fall of 1977, more than 8,000 Christians from 370 churches were mobilized for Here's Life, Taiwan, an evangelistic campaign designed to saturate an entire city with the gospel through trained lay men and women in a concentrated period of time. As a result of the momentum first initiated by the training center, major campaigns were mounted in 15 key cities of the Republic of China, the island's three television stations broadcast the gospel nationwide to millions, and more than 64,000 responded personally by telephone, mail or box coupons. What a dramatic demonstration of God's blessing on our training program!

The results are just as dramatic when we narrow down the account to the far-reaching effect which one individual can have, transformed by Jesus Christ and trained to share Him and disciple others.

I met such a high school student while speaking at a Leadership Training Institute in Malaysia in 1972. Her great heart for God was apparent, for she had traveled 110 miles to attend this training in Ipoh. Afterward, she went home to Penang and challenged her brother and friends to attend the next training. At the next LTI, there were her brother and eight of her friends!

After four years as a student leader at the University of Malaysia, that same young lady is responsible for leading scores of students to Christ and for discipling them. On a recent visit to Malaysia, she told me, "After graduation, the only natural thing for me to do is serve Christ in a full-time capacity."

I think also of Geogi, a student in Kerala, a state of India. This schoolboy attended an LTI a few months after he had become a Christian, and some time later one of the Indian staff members visited Geogi's school.

When he arrived, the teacher of Geogi's class led the staff member to his private room, took a Four Spiritual Laws booklet from his shelf and said, "Please teach me also how to use this booklet. I am not sure what you have done to Geogi, but he is really a changed person since he attended your camp. He has improved a lot in his studies, his behavior has changed dramatically, and he is sharing his faith with others through these Four Laws. If Geogi can share, I also can, so I want to study the 'how to's' of it."

Later that afternoon, Geogi shared the Four Spiritual Laws with the entire class. Among the 45 students present, 34, including Hindus and Muslims, indicated their decision for Jesus Christ.

Perhaps one of the more graphic demonstrations of spiritual multiplication which I have witnessed was given at a breakfast program which Dr. Bill Bright and I were attending to help launch Here's Life, Manila in March of 1976.

We were transfixed as a chain of students from the Manila's University of the East stood and shared with this group of pastors and lay leaders how spiritual multiplication was happening on their campus.

The series began with a student named Max, who stated: "Last year I heard how to invite Jesus Christ into my life and be used to introduce others to Him personally. At the present time, through a process called spiritual multiplication, 68 guys from the University of the East are being discipled by me or one of my disciples. I personally am discipling nine students in my cell group. One of those nine students is Tom, whom I introduced to Christ last year."

Tom continued, "When Max shared with me how I could become involved in spiritual multiplication, I really got excited. Now I have several groups started with a total of 17 students involved. Robert is one of those students."

Robert took over: "As one of Tom's disciples, I am learning more about how I can help build others in the Christian life. So far, I have a discovery group of three members. Ogie is one of my group members."

Ogie went on, "Robert shared with me how I can know Christ in a personal way. He is also following me up and has taught me how I can share with Rusl, and now I am following him up."

Rusl concluded, "I have only been a Christian for a few months, since Ogie shared the Four Spiritual Laws booklet with me. But I have already caught a vision of how I can be used to reach others, and I am discipling two guys from the University of the East at this time."

When the students finished, Dr. Bright looked at me, his eyes sparkling, and said, "That is the most exciting thing I have ever heard."

This is how, with singleness of purpose, a movement is being built in Asia — a movement designed to train Spirit-filled men and women to multiply themselves spiritually into the lives of others.

Personal Application

May I ask if you really know how to introduce a person to Christ and then how to disciple that individual effectively? Perhaps this chapter has shown you that spiritual multiplication can be a possibility — maybe even through your life. But let me remind you that you will never be a spiritual multiplier until you begin to obey Christ's command to win and disciple others. If you are an average Christian, like me, this will not come naturally; you need to be trained.

Within a few hours, you can be trained to introduce another to Christ. It takes only a few additional hours to begin to learn to disciple others. Are you willing?

Then I suggest that you immediately begin to explore opportunities to be trained in evangelism and discipleship. These can probably be found right in your own church or city. You may also want to contact our ministry through your local telephone directory for information on the next Campus Crusade training in your area.

CHAPTER SEVEN

An Impossible Dream

While journeying by automobile through the state of Kerala in South India one day, I decided to conduct an experiment. Seated in the front seat beside the driver, with an excellent view of the road on all sides, I wanted to clock the amount of time on this 150-mile trip I was out of sight of a person walking along the highway.

But it never happened. Not once, during five hours of steady driving, did I lose sight of at least one person.

I was to discover that this is the story of India. Masses and masses of people, wherever you look. With 680 million people, India is so densely populated that it contains nearly 20% of the world's entire population.

How well I remember my first visit to India in 1968, when I had to struggle with feelings of claustrophobia for the first time in my life. I was surrounded constantly by people, and I felt strangely helpless. Every night I would come back to my hotel room and ask, "God, can this country ever be reached for You? It seems to be an impossible dream...

* * *

In November of 1968, India Campus Crusade for Christ could scarcely be called a ministry. In fact, when I first met with our young director in Kerala, we were not sure whether we should laugh, cry or simply run away from consideration of fulfilling the Great Commission in India.

There we sat, two "nobodies" so far as evangelical circles in India were concerned. I was on my very first trip through Asia at the time, and my mind was spinning like a top as I tried to take in all that I was seeing and hearing. Thomas Abraham was likewise unknown — a young seminary graduate just returned to his homeland after several years in the United States.

But nevertheless, Thomas and I had the audacity to ignore all the odds, and we dreamed the impossible for India. We started to talk, pray and plan about the eventual training of hundreds of thousands of Indians ... about incorporating every available means of mass communication ... about seeing the millions of India confronted with the love and claims of Christ in our own generation. We knew we were ordinary men, but we determined to believe God in an extraordinary way.

I was soon to see God's wisdom in singling out Thomas Abraham to become the director of Campus Crusade in India.

Although Thomas grew up in a Christian home in South India, he had viewed Christianity as an empty ritual through his teenage years. When he entered the university, he became an avid Marxist and for several years devoted himself to perpetuating the Communist cause in India. But he eventually became disillusioned with Marxism, concluding that violent revolutions merely replace one set of problems with another.

Late in his university studies, the spiritual truths he had been taught by a godly father and mother began to penetrate his mind. When he heard the Word of God preached and learned how to experience a living relationship with Jesus Christ, he committed his life to Christ and received Him as Savior and Lord.

Several years later, Thomas entered Western Conservative Baptist Theological Seminary in the United States, where he was to graduate with highest honors. At that time, Thomas confirms, "I became quite satisfied with my life there in Portland, Ore. I was attending school, operating a printing business, and traveling up and down the west coast of the United States speaking at Bible conferences." He admits, "One thing that was *not* in my plan was for my wife, Molly, and me to return to India!"

But God had a different plan, and in the summer of 1967 Thomas attended a Campus Crusade conference in southern California. "I agreed to come as an observer, and a skeptical one at that!" he explains wryly. He relates that when the staff went to the beaches to share their faith in Christ with sunbathers, he went along in unbelief. However, he decided to experiment with the evangelistic method he had been taught at the conference, so he hesitantly approached people and explained to them how they could know Christ personally.

That afternoon on the beach, Thomas introduced more people to the Lord than he had ever led to Christ during his

"Thomas and I had the audacity to ignore all the odds, and we dreamed the impossible for India."

Bailey and Campus Crusade national director in India, Thomas Abraham, discuss strategy to reach the state of Kerala with the gospel.

"How I thank God every day for our staff leaders in the Orient — for their total availability to God, and for the privilege I have to serve the Lord Jesus Christ with them."

Bailey with two staff members, Thailand national director Somdee Poosawtsee (left) and Jerry Sharpless, Here's Life Asia strategy coordinator.

entire life! "My theological training had been thorough," he says, "but I had never before seen the results of communicating my faith in Christ directly with others."

He recalls, "During the next year my motives and desires began to change. For the first time, a spiritual burden for the people of India began to be generated in my heart. When Dr. Bright challenged me to return to India and invest my life on the front line of the battle in reaching my country for Christ, I was ready."

Fifteen months after he had walked on that southern California beach, Thomas and Molly Abraham were back in India. As I met with them that first time in Kerala, we knew that although we "dreamed big," we would have to begin small.

Thomas's simple plan was to start a campus ministry in the state of Kerala, where he and Molly would daily confront college students with the claims of Christ. He later explained, "The first day I went on campus by myself, not certain what would happen. The first student I talked to received Christ. I got so excited that I went back home to tell Molly that aggressive evangelism worked in India!" And so they began, obediently sharing the claims of Christ with one student after another.

With such a humble beginning, many of our grandiose plans seemed unrealistic. But God was to put flesh on the bones of those skeleton plans in a miraculous way over the next eight years.

Gradually, through students and laymen they had won and discipled for Christ, Thomas and Molly saw their little staff team grow. "Eight of the first 12 people who joined staff were won to the Lord through my personal ministry," Thomas recalls. But to saturate Kerala's 22 million people scattered in nearly three million homes with the gospel, they needed a massive force of trained Christians.

From 1969 through 1975, the India Campus Crusade staff continued faithfully to win, build and send for Christ on an ever-widening scale. Then in August of 1975, Bishop John of the Church of South India joined our staff. Through his support, Lay Institutes for Evangelism were scheduled all across Kerala in the next few months, and by the end of the year, 267 churches were committed to and involved in the saturation of Kerala.

An Impossible Dream

At that point, we had in Kerala an army of at least 30,000 trained Christian workers. "It became clear to us at the close of 1975," states Thomas, "that our target date for saturating Kerala should be the end of 1976."

In addition, 920 local evangelists — both volunteers and full-time church workers — received training to participate in the saturation. In turn, they recruited and trained more than 15,000 members of their prayer groups to be a part of the saturation!

A brochure designed specifically for the Indian culture was printed by the millions to present testimonies, pictures and the Four Spiritual Laws. The two major newspapers in the Malayalam language printed the brochure, with the editor of the largest daily commenting, "I have never seen anything that captures the mind of the ordinary person like this brochure does."

During 1976, workers representing every major church denomination, colleges, Christian organizations, high schools and prayer groups methodically went about the task of visiting every home in Kerala to present the claims of Christ using the Four Spiritual Laws. By October, more than 40,000 Christian workers were involved in the house-to-house strategy.

Comprehensive voter lists of Kerala's 11 major districts were used to give visitation assignments to the volunteers. When it was ascertained through weekly reports submitted by all volunteers that an area had been completely saturated, our staff members went to confirm their figures.

Thomas himself personally made random surveys in hundreds of homes, and he never found a home that had not been contacted! "In every home where we inquired," Thomas states, "someone had been there to share the claims of Christ." The usual evidence was a copy of the special Four Laws brochure still in the home!

To help reach those not at home when the workers called, large evangelistic meetings were held in all 11 districts of Kerala during the last three months of 1976, drawing a total attendance of more than two million people. Some churches discontinued their usual Sunday afternoon youth programs to allow their young people to participate in the visitation or assist with publicity for the public meetings.

On December 31, 1976, Thomas was able to say, "We praise

God for the completed task of saturating our Jerusalem with the good news!"

By the grace of God, 99% of the 2,700,000 homes in Kerala had been blanketed with the gospel, and more than 1.4 million people indicated that they received Christ through person-to-person presentations. Another 380,028 indicated decisions for Christ at the public meetings.

Here is a statistical review of what has been considered to be one of the largest saturation programs ever to be conducted in the history of Christianity in any country of the world:

THE PARAMETER

Population of Kerala	22,000,000
Number of Homes in Kerala	2,700,000
Average Family Size	7
Number of Major Cities	11

THE RESOURCES

Full-time India Staff	51
Total Trained in 1976	37,425
Total Number of Churches Involved	267
Total Number of People Mobilized to Help With Here's Life, Kerala	43,309
Kerala Staff Members	38
Evangelists (Trained)	720
Evangelists Employed Full-time	200
Laymen (Reporting to Churches)	6,675
Students (Reporting to Staff)	19,920
Prayer Group Members (Reporting to Evangelists)	15,756
TOTAL	43,309

THE RESULTS

Number Attending Public Meetings	Over 2 million
Decisions Indicated for Christ at Public Meetings	Over 350,000
Number of Person-to-person Presentations of Christ	7,741,863
Decisions Indicated for Christ Through Person-to-person Presentations	1,470,954

Just eight years after Thomas Abraham took his first step of faith toward the saturation of his nation with the message

An Impossible Dream

"By the grace of God, 99% of the 2,700,000 homes in Kerala had been blanketed with the gospel."

A Here's Life, Kerala village evangelist reads through the Four Spiritual Laws booklet with a motorcyclist. A total of 43,309 trained workers were mobilized for the campaign. The result: 1,470,954 indicated decisions for Christ through person to person gospel presentations.

of God's love and forgiveness, he saw the first of India's 22 states completely saturated for Christ!

The remarkable story of Kerala helps us believe God for even bigger plans — reaching the rest of India and all of Asia with the gospel.

To build a movement, to gain momentum, to cultivate the confidence of Christian leaders on a continent as sprawling and diverse as Asia takes a lot of time and creative energy. Our hearts are full of praise to God for what He has done through our Asian staff in the last decade, and we are full of anticipation for the future.

The following listing of our Asian ministries shows how God in His timing has brought staff into this ministry. Clearly, an impossible dream is coming true!

COUNTRY	YEAR ESTABLISHED
South Korea	1958
Japan	1962
Taiwan (ROC)	1964
Philippines	1965
Sri Lanka	1967
India	1968
Malaysia	1968
Indonesia	1968
Australia	1968
Vietnam	1970
Thailand	1971
Singapore	1971
Hong Kong	1972
Cambodia	1973
Marshall Islands	1973
Burma	1973
New Zealand	1973
Solomon Islands	1973
Guam	1973
Fiji	1974
Tonga	1974
Bangladesh	1975
Nepal	1975
Macau	1975
New Guinea	1977
Cook Islands	1977
New Hebrides	1977

An Impossible Dream

Personal Application

Nowhere in Asia did our ministry begin with a large mass of willing, excited, trained people. It has always started with just a few . . . often just one available Christian who dared to believe God for an "impossible" dream. Thomas Abraham is one such faithful man in India whom God appointed to plan and then help implement a way to reach his Jerusalem. And it literally happened.

Are you waiting for a special climate of spiritual awakening to happen in your church, community or area of influence? If so, I believe that you are limiting God and the possibilities He has for you. Right now God is taking ordinary, available Christians all over the world and multiplying their ministry to help reach thousands and even entire countries.

I challenge you, regardless of the spiritual circumstances in which you find yourself, to look at your Jerusalem from God's perspective. Let Him stretch your faith for the fulfillment of Christ's commission through *you*.

"I was seeing the awesome result of a vision that God had given to Dr. Joon Gon Kim."

Massive crowds like this carpeted Yoido Island, prompting Dr. Kim to call EXPLO '74, "the largest Christian gathering in history." According to police estimates, 1.3 million attended two evening mass rallies during the five-day conference.

CHAPTER EIGHT

Wet Feet for God

The rain was pelting down so hard that no one in his right mind should have been out of doors. Even though I wore a raincoat and huddled beneath my umbrella, I didn't have an article of dry clothing on me!

From a 30-foot platform, I watched a crowd of one million also very wet people. Most sat in rain puddles on the ground, listening intently to the news of God's love and forgiveness.

It was August of 1974, at EXPLO '74 in Seoul, Korea. I was seeing the awesome result of a vision that God had given to Dr. Joon Gon Kim, director of Korea Campus Crusade for Christ.

My mind raced back two years before, when I sat listening to Dr. Kim in a stadium at EXPLO '72, a national training congress on evangelism in Dallas, Tex. Before 85,000 delegates, Dr. Kim shared what God was doing in Korea.

Suddenly his mood changed, and he began to pour out his vision of what he believed God wanted to do in Korea. He concluded by stating that the next EXPLO would be held in Seoul, Korea, during the summer of 1974 — and more than 300,000 delegates would attend!

Perplexed, my wife whispered to me, "You haven't mentioned that to me before." Since I was director of affairs for our ministry in Asia and the South Pacific, the announcement shouldn't have surprised me. But turning to Elizabeth, I whispered back, "I just heard about it for the first time myself!"

Standing on that rain-soaked platform in Seoul two years later, there was no question in my mind why one million people were sitting there . . . and why 323,419 had registered as EXPLO '74 delegates. The reason was all wrapped up in the faith of a man named Dr. Joon Gon Kim, who wasn't afraid to get his feet wet . . . !

* * *

God spoke very clearly to Dr. Joon Gon Kim that June afternoon in Dallas. The vision He gave Dr. Kim for a massive conference on evangelism in Korea was bestowed very deliberately, I believe, on this particular Korean gentleman.

I say that because Dr. Kim expects God to do great things. This faith typifies his daily life. It is so simple that it's extraordinary . . . and that has ministered to me deeply on a number of occasions.

As one of God's chosen instruments, filling a vital role to help reach Korea and the world for Christ, Dr. Kim's background is interwoven with his heartbeat for the Lord Jesus Christ.

By his own admission, Dr. Kim was a nominal Christian 30 years ago. Brought up in a strict Confucianist home, he first heard about Jesus Christ as a third-grade lad in primary school. During his teenage years, he became interested in Christianity and sought out a Christian church to attend. It was there he committed his life to Christ, becoming active in the church throughout his school years and young married life.

Then came the Korean War. "The starting point of my real Christian life began when I faced persecution and death under the Communist occupation," testifies Dr. Kim. He and his family took refuge on Chido Island at the southern tip of Korea. Native partisans and guerrillas began to invade and confiscate property, killing indivduals and families without trial. No law existed, and all means of escape from the island were cut off.

At family devotions one night, Dr. Kim's devout Christian wife prayed that all of them might be prepared to meet the death which seemed inevitable. That same night, Dr. Kim and his wife and father were awakened about 2 a.m. by pounding on their door. They were trussed up and taken to the mountains to be killed.

"Our executioners were fellow villagers who had joined the Communists," recalls Dr. Kim, "and they began with my father. Just a stone's throw away from me, my father was struck on the head several times and fell dead. Then my wife, trying to keep back her tears, said goodbye to me and said she would see me in heaven. Right before my eyes, she was brutally killed."

Dr. Kim was beaten repeatedly with a club until he lost consciousness and was left for dead after two more beatings.

"Dr. Kim expects God to do great things. This faith typifies his daily life. It is so simple that it's extraordinary."

Bailey and Dr. Kim confer in the shade during a training institute in 1977.

More than 2,000 people were murdered that night with clubs, stones and bamboo spears, but Dr. Kim remained alive. He rushed home for his four-year-old daughter, and together they fled into the mountains.

"I am told that I was the only survivor among those whom the Communists had marked for death," he states. Later, additional attempts were made on his life — from the time he felt a sword blade at his throat to the day he was tied in a sack to be thrown from a cliff into the sea. But each time God intervened and spared his life.

Dragging with exhaustion, Dr. Kim and his daughter managed to keep running and hiding for three weeks in mountain caves along the coast. Dr. Kim recalls, "I was almost dead physically and could not even move to help my little girl who was dying from hunger and longing for her mother. My consciousness came and went for days at a time.

"I was also dead psychologically, because I had no hope. There seemed to be no way of escape.

"But the most serious thing was my spiritual condition. I had stopped praying or expecting God to answer, and I had no desire even for eternal life. I lost sight of God, and within my soul I was complaining and trying to cut myself off from Him. I experienced the total despair and darkness of spiritual death, which was a feeling of complete separation from God. It was unbearable."

Then a strange thing happened. "Suddenly I realized that my lips had begun to move in prayer to God," relates Dr. Kim. "That prayer was begun on my lips by the Holy Spirit, and it ended in my heart. At that moment I passed from death to life. As I turned to my Savior, great peace and joy sprang from my heart like a river. My hatred for the Communists vanished, and there burned in my heart a desire to please God, to glorify His name and to do His will.

"I began to pray for the Communist whom I hated most — the leader who had beaten me and killed my family. I called his name and asked for God's grace, love and forgiveness of his sin." As Dr. Kim prayed by name for all his enemies, his strength was restored.

Experiencing a new freedom from fear, hatred and death, Dr. Kim was able to stand up, take his daughter by the hand and leave the cave. He headed straight toward his enemy's home. When the Communist came to the door, he was greatly startled by the appearance of a man whom he believed to be dead!

Dr. Kim gently, bravely explained that he had come in the name of Jesus to express his love for him. Overwhelmed, the man and his wife hid Dr. Kim and his daughter in their home that night. As Dr. Kim proceeded to share with his would-be murderer about the love of God and forgiveness of sin through Jesus Christ, this Communist leader wept over his sins and became a new man in Christ.

At great risk, he continued to feed and protect Dr. Kim for several days, and in time, more than 30 of his fellow Communists in that village made decisions for Christ. This man is now a faithful witness for Christ, serving as a deacon in a small Presbyterian Church. "We still pray for one another every day," comments Dr. Kim.

Can you imagine the faith, courage and supernatural love that it took for Dr. Kim to go back into that village, find the murderers of his father and his wife, and confront them with the love of Jesus Christ? Obviously, that session with the Lord in the cave was the turning point in Dr. Kim's life. Since then, he has moved forward to be used of God as very few other people have been used in this century.

To be quite honest, Dr. Kim's vision for a week-long conference for 300,000 delegates had filled many of us with a skepticism that bordered on unbelief. How could such a mammoth Christian gathering be accomplished in a Buddhist country?

The Korean Campus Crusade staff, in particular, were filled with negative thoughts. Finally, Dr. Kim assembled his entire staff in order to confront and deal with their unbelief. On a blackboard, they listed every opposition that came to their minds. When they finished, they had named 76 major reasons they believed EXPLO '74 could not happen.

Many of the barriers involved the logistical problems — housing, food preparation, finances, weather, transportation, etc. Imagine preparing rice for 300,000 people twice a day! And where were they going to sleep at night? And on top of it all, they would have to operate on a very limited budget.

When they could not think of another problem to list, Dr. Kim asked them a very strategic question: "Is God big enough to overcome these problems?" The staff then realized they were faced with a decision: to believe God to overcome each one of these objections, or to give up because of the circumstances.

They decided to trust God, and through the next year and a half, they saw God overcome all of the 76 barriers except one — the weather. It rained two nights. In fact, it poured! But God used this to demonstrate to the world the commitment of the Korean Christians. No one who was there will ever forget the sight of more than a million people sitting in the rain to hear men talk about Jesus!

The other problems were all solved in due time. The government allowed public school classrooms to be used for housing, along with the pitching of one of the largest tent cities ever seen. To solve the food problem, God used Dr. Kim to invent a new kind of rice cooker to prepare the rice!

As a result of the faith of Dr. Kim and his staff, more than 323,000 delegates registered for the conference. Some of the evening evangelistic meetings drew more than one and a half million people to hear how they could know God in a personal way.

EXPLO '74 also served as a faith catalyst to Christians all across the Orient. They saw God do the impossible in Korea — something that very few human minds had ever considered possible. The faith of visiting delegates from 78 other countries was increased, and they began to believe God to accomplish similar impossibilities in their own lands.

Shortly before this congress, government statistics showed slightly over three million Protestant Christians in South Korea. Four years later, the official figures had doubled to more than seven million Protestants in South Korea!

EXPLO '74 will always remain one of the greatest lessons on faith I have personally experienced. But my thinking about faith began to crystalize in early 1969, while I was in the unpleasant state of lying flat on my back in the hospital for several months at the end of that first trip to Asia.

At first, I was quite bitter about the situation, wondering, "Why did God allow something like this to happen to me?" Deep in my heart, I began to fear that I would never be able to travel again or live in Asia. All the time I kept hearing that still small voice of the Lord saying, "Why don't you trust Me?

Why don't you trust Me?" But I kept excusing myself, answering, "Lord, You don't understand. I'm so sick!"

God put into my hands in those days a book by Norman Grubb entitled *God Unlimited*. Mr. Grubb used in his book a word which cannot be found in the dictionary — the word "unfaith." As a result of seeing that word for the first time, my faith life changed radically. It helped me greatly in understanding my situation to use the proper antonym for faith — "unfaith" or unbelief.

At that point I'd accepted the concept that faith is an act of the will — a deliberate decision to trust God. But suddenly I was faced with the reality that the opposite is also true! Unbelief, or unfaith as Mr. Grubb so bluntly put it, is also very much an act of my will — not a passive occurrence, or something that snuck up on me. Lying there in the hospital, I had actually decided that I was *not* going to believe in God!

That afternoon, I decided to start believing God. This decision, along with many subsequent acts of my will, was a significant event in my Christian life — perhaps more valuable to me during the last 10 years than almost anything else I've experienced.

I was surprised to learn that the more we grow in Christ, the more we face battles. For me, this has included my constant battle with unbelief. Over and over again, I have opportunity to wrestle with the question, "Will I believe God to raise me above the circumstances of the present situation, and will I give Him opportunity to use me as He sees fit in the future?"

I tend to respond negatively to a new situation rather than positively. My immediate response to change or new ideas is often, "It won't work!" or "We've never done it that way before!" So I have learned that I must exercise faith in order to develop a positive attitude. I must refuse to look at circumstances from a human perspective; instead I focus on God Himself and His promises. I cannot expect God to use me effectively until I first come to grips with unbelief in my own life and ministry.

Planning has been a tremendous help to me in dealing with unbelief and trusting God to do things that seem impossible. Whenever I'm faced with great, imposing situations that my finite mind just cannot comprehend, I try to establish intermediate or short-term goals to help me obtain a better grasp of the situation.

This is especially true when I'm in a situation where I have to believe God for something that may not take place for several years. God will need to perform a number of miracles in order to bring this situation about and to achieve the objectives. It's really too big for me to comprehend. So, instead of quitting, sitting down and doing nothing because the task is beyond us, I begin to plan. I map out a course of action, putting down the necessary steps from where I am today to where I want to be ultimately, several years away.

My next step is to establish short-range goals and objectives on a monthly, semi-annual or annual basis. I watch God do miracle after miracle to meet these "little" goals, and my faith has a chance to grow. I find myself as a result able to believe God for even greater things, so I can continue to be obedient in moving toward my major goal.

The Book of Joshua contains a meaningful reminder to me. In the third chapter, we find the children of Israel facing their second opportunity to enter the Promised Land. A generation earlier, their parents had been given a chance to enter, but they refused to believe God was bigger than the circumstances, so they had wandered in the desert for 40 years.

As this new group of Israelites came to the Jordan River, they faced a set of circumstances just as difficult as their parents had faced. Again the question arose, "Are we going to believe God?" The immediate obstacle was the Jordan River, swollen at flood season.

The Bible tells us that the priests who were carrying the ark stepped into the river, and they were ankle-deep in the current before the waters parted. They had to step into the water before they saw what God was going to do for them. The water didn't reach their knees or even their waist, only their ankles. All that God required of them was to "get their feet wet!"

That's exactly what He requires of us today. I am constantly asking myself, "Bailey, are you willing to get your feet wet? Are you willing to trust God and take that first step of faith, regardless of the consequences?"

Sometimes it takes awhile for me to start moving. But when I do decide to get my feet wet in obedience, taking one step at a time, God goes to work and miracles begin to happen.

When God impressed Dr. Bill Bright to believe that the world would be saturated with the gospel by 1980, I had to face up to a gigantic faith barrier. Our ministry had actually accepted the prayer target of 1980 for the fulfillment of the Great Commission in every nation of the world! "Am I going to believe God for this?" I asked myself continually. I applied faith in my life in relation to this 1980 goal — "getting my feet wet" — by taking the initial step.

In 1971, we did our first major planning on the part we believed God would have our ministry play in helping to reach all of Asia by 1980. We looked seriously at our existing ministry and began planning ahead through 1980.

At that time, we had fewer than 100 staff ministering in nine countries in the present Asia-South Pacific area of affairs. After we had put on paper what we were asking God to do through our ministry, it was so far beyond my own mental comprehension that I was stricken with unbelief. I felt helpless. Then I remembered that my responsibility was to take one step of faith at a time; so that's what we did. We began concentrating on the intermediate goals and objectives we'd set in our planning session. Our initial plans called for our present staff to increase in number at a rate of 100% each year for the next eight years. By 1980, we were to have 12,000 full-time staff members in Asia.

During the subsequent years, God has changed that plan radically. He has shown us clearly that it is not His desire for us to have nearly that number of full-time staff. However, what God did during the first two years following our first step of faith was remarkable: Our staff increased 100% each of those years, and our faith grew tremendously.

Another step in our plans was that by 1975 we would be ministering in every country of Asia where political doors were open for us. We met that goal, and today our staff numbers about 900 in 27 nations of Asia and the South Pacific. We had crossed another hurdle, and now we're able to believe God for the next step as we keep moving toward our ultimate goal of helping to fulfill the Great Commission in Asia by 1980.

As I have watched God work over the past eight years, my faith has increased to the point where 1980 seems much more realistic. Because I've seen God answer our prayers and fulfill our intermediate goals and objectives, I can now trust Him to accomplish our long-range goals.

For years the greatest faith barrier we faced in the Orient was reaching the Chinese mainland for Christ. One-fourth of the entire world's population resides there, yet there is no freedom to preach the gospel. For years, the question kept running through my mind, "How does China relate to the fulfillment of the Great Commission in our generation?"

One morning several years ago, God began asking *me* a question: "What would Campus Crusade do if the doors of the Chinese mainland were open today?" For weeks I pondered that question over and over, until I honestly concluded that if the doors suddenly opened, there would be very little change in what we were doing. Obviously, we were not prepared for the doors to open!

I was impressed with the fact that almost all of Christendom was unprepared to go into China. We were all praying for the doors of China to open, but we were totally unprepared to enter once they did! We were not "getting our feet wet" by taking initial steps of preparation.

So our Chinese staff and other leaders began to pray, asking God what we needed to do to be ready. God began showing us that we already had many open doors, with Chinese scattered all over the Orient. Most of the countries in Asia are open and responsive to the gospel, but most of the people in these nations have never heard how to know Christ in a personal way.

Thus, our immediate responsibility was clearly to take the gospel to the people in these "open" countries. Our intermediate goal toward reaching mainland China then became to share the gospel with the Chinese in these "open" countries and train them to become spiritual multipliers — confident that God would continue to open doors.

Our strategies were accelerated by many different means, the foremost of which was the Here's Life strategy. Through Here's Life we moved as rapidly as possible into major cities of the Orient where large groups of Chinese reside.

By the fall of 1978, Here's Life, Asia had taken place in every major city in the Orient where significant numbers of Chinese live. Then thousands of believers were challenged to prepare themselves to enter the mainland when the doors opened. By means of shortwave radio, evangelistic messages and our introductory training in discipleship were being prepared to begin broadcasting all over China by July 1, 1979. Thousands of prayer cells were forming all over the world to pray for what we were convinced would be a great spiritual harvest in China.

It was not a shock to our ministry, therefore, when at the close of 1978 it became apparent that the political and economic doors of China — closed tight for over 30 years — were beginning a dramatic swing open. We had stepped out in faith, getting our feet wet. And finally, in late 1978, Elizabeth and I were privileged to visit China ourselves, to see the situation there firsthand. God has already done so many miracles through these initial steps that today I have no difficulty in believing Him for the fulfillment of our Lord's Great Commission on the entire Chinese mainland.

Very simply, God honors our faith and obedience to commit ourselves to His plans, commands and promises. We stepped out, and the impossible is becoming reality!

Personal Application

Every day you face decisions to exercise faith or unfaith. Is there any area of your life that has become a faith barrier for you? Perhaps you fell into the same subconscious trap that I did — excusing your unbelief by the circumstances or a "normal" negative response to change.

The decision is yours. I simply repeat Dr. Kim's quiet question to the Korean staff: "Is God big enough to overcome your problems?"

Ask yourself: "Am I, as an act of my will, willing to believe God and exercise my faith; or am I, as an act of my will, *not* willing to believe God and therefore exercise my unfaith?"

The Lord will honor your faith and obedience when you step out and get your feet wet!

CHAPTER NINE

When God Opens the Door

Dear Mr. Bailey Marks,

First of all we would like to [apologize for writing] this letter by hand. As you know, in this situation we don't have electricity to use our English typewriter. Within 48 hours we have electricity only 2 or 3 hours.

Now all classes are closed (college, high school, private school). We are making contacts at our place. The situation is very hard. We cannot say what will happen for the next day, next week, but we are happy to live and to die for our Lord Jesus Christ.

We have decided to serve our Lord Jesus Christ until our last minute of lives in reaching Cambodia for Him. Please continue to pray for our strength both physically and spiritually. We do hope that if [it is] God's will we can see you once again before we die, or we'll meet each other in heaven.

Please give our regards to all our beloved staff of Campus Crusade for Christ around the world.

Yours in our Lord Jesus Christ,
Huong & Samoeun and baby

* * *

It was the last letter I received from our very dear young staff couple in Cambodia. For several hours after I received it, I wept and prayed in real agony of heart.

I knew that I had to thank God for the situation — that this choice couple had decided to remain in their homeland even as it fell to Communism. But I had a difficult time to rejoice in the Lord, as the sobering facts of the Khmer Rouge revolution began to escape the sealed borders of Cambodia.

News magazines and the wire services began to hint that with abrupt cruelty, the new Communist regime had forced the entire urban population of the country to abandon the cities and revert to a primitive, rural society. In the process, an estimated two million Cambodians died of malnutrition, starvation, disease, forced labor or execution. Religion, whether Christianity or the native Buddhism, was reviled as "reactionary," and places of worship were razed.

However, the Lord soon began to remind me of our completeness in Christ. The words of John 15:11 were of particular comfort and strength: "These things I have spoken to you, that My joy may be in you, and that your joy may be made full." I found my burden lifted only a few hours after I received Huong and Samoeun's letter, and I began to pray that they might experience this extraordinary, supernatural joy, even as I claimed it for myself.

As I was praying for them some time later, the promise of Revelation 3:7,8 seemed to have Huong and Samoeun's names written on it:

> "He who is holy, who is true . . . says this . . . Behold, I have put before you an open door which no one can shut!"

No one can shut a door which God has opened except God Himself! I rejoiced in that promise, for I had seen with my own eyes how God had opened the doors for His witness in Cambodia. Hearts there were truly prepared, and people were responding to the gospel. In the last months before Lon Nol's government fell, there was such a widespread turning to Christ that newspapers in the capital city of Phnom Penh were calling for government containment of Christianity. This in a land rated 97.5% Buddhist!

As I claimed that promise, I thought to myself, "The doors to Cambodia may have been closed by man, but no human government can close the doors to people's hearts!"

Throughout the next four years, God planted within my heart the confidence that amid the horror, destruction and probable religious persecution, there was another revolution at work in Cambodia — a spiritual revolution. I had very little information to document my convictions, apart from my knowledge of the moving of God's Spirit in Cambodia before the revolution.

I'd wanted to visit Cambodia since I first came to Asia. But at that time, during the latter part of Prince Sihanouk's reign, I wasn't permitted as a U.S. citizen to enter the country. So after the *coup d'état* in 1970, I quickly made preparations for

When God Opens the Door

my long-awaited trip to visit Cambodian Christians and missionaries.

God had brought me into contact with the Merle Gravens, Christian and Missionary Alliance missionaries who had served in Cambodia for many years until all American missionaries were deported in the early 1960's. During the interim years before they could return, Merle pastored a rapidly-growing church in the United States. Shortly after his church had sponsored a Lay Institute for Evangelism conducted by Campus Crusade, the doors to Cambodia re-opened. Gravens returned to Phnom Penh, at the request of the small Cambodian congregation there, and soon afterward Merle wrote to ask if our lay institute training could be given to the believers in Phnom Penh. At that time, there were an estimated 300 Protestant Christians in the entire country!

Within a matter of weeks I departed for Phnom Penh. My first impression, driving in from the airport, was an unforgettable surprise: Built by the French colonists, Phnom Penh was a beautiful city with pleasant, wide boulevards. It was exceptionally clean and well kept.

Then I began to meet the Christians. Such a loving, warm group of people — but oh, so small in number. One afternoon I sat down with 14 Christian students on their university campus to talk about starting a student ministry there. I was overwhelmed to learn that small circle represented 75% of all the born-again Christian college students in the nation! Yet that short time together provided the base for the great work of God's Spirit in Cambodia.

We talked for several hours through an interpreter, and then I asked, "What can Campus Crusade for Christ do to help you?" One young man, an agricultural engineering student, spoke up, "We understand that you can train people to witness. Would you come back and teach us how to share our faith in Christ with others?"

The young man who asked that question was Vek Huong Taing. He looked like an ordinary Khmer student to me, but today I consider him one of the most outstanding young men I have ever met. His remarkable story exemplifies what God will do in the life of an ordinary person who says to the Lord, "I'm available."

Several months later, in response to repeated invitations

from the believers, I returned with Bud and Elizabeth Newbold to conduct our first training conference on evangelism in Cambodia. As part of the training, we took a group of 42 frightened Christians out to witness in the beautiful parks of Phnom Penh. So far as we know, that was the first such aggressive witness for Christ in the history of Cambodia.

That afternoon, 99 Cambodian Buddhists who heard about the claims of Jesus Christ — most for the first time in their lives — prayed by faith and invited Jesus to come into their hearts. A number of these new believers came back to the church that evening with the individuals who had shared the Four Spiritual Laws with them, commenting: "I have always been looking for peace and purpose . . . I wanted the real answers to life . . . This afternoon through the Four Spiritual Laws in our Khmer language, I invited Christ into my life."

During the next few years, God was to use the combined efforts of World Vision International and Campus Crusade for Christ, under the leadership of the Christian and Missionary Alliance, to move in a most unusual way in Cambodia. Following the principle of national leadership, we frequently shared with Cambodian pastors and missionaries our desire to find some national staff to direct our work in Cambodia.

The Rev. Gene Hall and others who worked closely with our ministry recommended that we challenge that young student, Vek Huong Taing, to join our staff. At first, I didn't agree with them. During our first lay institute in Cambodia, Huong had been in charge of our training group. But from my brief exposure to him, I wasn't sure that he was the person to head up a movement of aggressive evangelism and discipleship.

It seemed that every time we had lectures or seminars, Huong was out getting tea and cookies ready, or preparing the noon meal. And on the afternoon of witnessing, Huong was in the kitchen fixing submarine sandwiches! Besides, he didn't know any English, and that would be necessary for him to enroll at our Manila training base.

However, as I continued to correspond regarding Huong's application for staff, the daily newspapers were filling with accounts of the war in Cambodia. One morning in Manila, my colleague, Bud Newbold, and I read in the newspaper that military trucks were rumbling through the streets of Phnom

Penh, picking up any young men they saw of fighting age. These young men were then driven to a military base, put in uniforms and sent out to fight in the rice paddies.

Mr. Newbold and I stared at each other, knowing we must make a decision. Huong was then 24 years old — just the right age to be sent into battle. We finally concluded: "Well, let's go ahead and invite him to join us. He'll probably never be able to get out of Cambodia to come to Manila for training, anyway!"

How very wrong we were! And how thankful I am that God proved us to be so wrong!

We cabled our acceptance invitation to Huong, and our missionary contacts reassured us that Huong was studying to acquire a good grasp of English before coming to Manila for training.

Three months later, I was astonished to receive a telegram saying that Huong *and* his new bride, Samoeun, would be arriving in Manila in a few days. I had to wait in suspense to learn how God had opened the doors to enable them to leave Cambodia.

Later Huong and Samoeun told us how they had marched into the Foreign Affairs Office in Phnom Penh and requested passports to leave the country. Questioned over and over again as to their reasons, Huong boldly explained why to the government officials, most of whom were Buddhists.

"We are Christians," he said, "and an international Christian organization has invited us to join their staff. We must go to the Philippines to be trained. Then we will return to Cambodia to tell other people how they can become Christians."

Any young man who could walk in Cambodia was being given a rifle and a uniform. But Huong and Samoeun were granted their passports and exit permits, and they left for Manila!

However, when Elizabeth and I met them at Manila International Airport, it was soon evident that they were not at all coherent in English. As we drove home together in almost total silence, I thought, "How will our trainers ever train them? Even though they're here by a miracle, it will take another one for them to communicate!"

Then their determination began to shine through. Resolving to learn the English language, they covenanted to stop speaking their mother tongue of Khmer to each other. Even in the privacy of their own room, they spoke only English. Within 60 days, Huong was not only sharing Christ in English with university students, but he was also standing up in classrooms to present the gospel! A few weeks later, Samoeun was doing the same.

After completing their six months of training and representing Cambodia at EXPLO '74 in Korea, Huong and Samoeun came to my office in the fall of 1974, ready to return home. I cautioned them, "You know the political situation in your country better than I do. The chances of Cambodia's survival do not look good." I explained that no one would think less of them if they decided to remain in Manila until the situation in Cambodia became more stable. In the meantime, they could serve the Lord through our ministry in the Philippines.

At that time, Huong was an "old" man of 25. Lovingly, yet sternly, he looked at me and said, "I am Khmer. You brought me here and trained me to go back and give the gospel to my people. They have had fewer opportunities to hear about Christ than almost any other country in the world.

"I could never stay here when my people are dying every day without Jesus," he concluded. I could say no more, and I thanked them for their answer.

They returned home to Phnom Penh in October. Shortly before Christmas that year, I visited them to see the fruit of their young ministry. All over the city, I was continually introduced to new believers who had come to know the Lord through their witness.

"I have never seen a young man so bold to share his faith as Huong," the Rev. Gene Hall told me. He had observed that Huong and Samoeun not only knew how to win people to Christ and disciple them, but in those few months they also had already trained 30 strong disciples to do the same!

The missionaries in Phnom Penh also pointed out the phenomenal rate of church growth there in the capital city. Pointing to a city map, Rev. Hall indicated 32 groups of Christians that had met across the city the previous Sunday. I recalled my first visit to Phnom Penh three years before, when only three groups of believers were meeting in the city!

But through my joy, I knew that the days of freedom in Cambodia were numbered. Each night during my visit, my bed would vibrate from the bombing and artillery barrage all around the city. Several times I stood at my window at night, watching the sky light up from repeated explosions.

Shortly before I left, I told Huong and Samoeun once again how much I loved them and how thankful I was for them. I gave them what turned out to be a final chance to fly out with me and leave their war-torn country. As I expected, their reply was firm, identical to their first answer: they wanted to serve Christ in Cambodia with their last breath.

As I flew out that day, my thoughts were sober. I knew I probably would not see them again for a very long time. "Maybe not before we reach heaven," I admitted.

From that point on, I could only pray . . . through the fall of Cambodia in April, 1975, and on through the next four years.

In fact, God reminded me so often to pray for them that finally I asked, "Lord, shall I keep praying?" If they were with the Lord, then I wanted His peace to accept that joyfully. But if God continued to lay it upon my heart to pray for them, then I had to believe they were still alive and boldly witnessing for Christ in Cambodia.

The Lord never did lift from me that burden to pray for Huong, Samoeun and their little son, born two months before Phnom Penh fell. So when word came, in late April of 1979, that all three of them had safely escaped across the border of Cambodia into Thailand, I was ecstatic but not surprised. I just didn't think that God would keep me praying for a dead family for four years!

The account of their miraculous odyssey across the jungles of Cambodia to freedom is a book in itself. I wept again as they shared with me much of the suffering, horror and persecution which they endured — but I have rejoiced at the triumph shining in their eyes as they have related God's great miracles and blessings through the four years of their captivity.*

While millions around them starved to death or were brutally executed, God miraculously preserved this couple alive for His service. He performed another miraculous sequence of events so that 12 days after they walked across the

---

*Read ORDEAL IN CAMBODIA, Here's Life Publishers, San Bernardino, CA. 92402.

border into Thailand, they were boarding a plane in Bangkok with me, flying to safety in the United States.

I can hardly wait to see what God will do through them in their "second lives," as Huong and Samoeun refer to the miracle of living through the Cambodian revolution. I know of no better way to explain their zeal and commitment than to quote Huong's question to the first staff member he met after escaping Cambodia: "How are we doing on the Great Commission?"

They are just another ordinary couple, stepping out into an extraordinary life for God. Through their simple availability, they have helped to pave the way for an ongoing spiritual revolution among Cambodia's millions.

Personal Application

There's a lot of talk among Christians about being available. Unfortunately, many people seem to think they are available if they stand in neutral, saying, "Lord, I'm ready to be used!"

To me, a Spirit-filled Christian who is available goes directly to God about a particular situation or course of action he or she should take. He seeks the counsel of others, if appropriate. Then he makes a decision on what to do, and he steps out in that direction.

Quite often, real availability involves a lot of hard work. But Jesus never said it would be easy. Huong and Samoeun faced some of the most difficult challenges that I've ever seen placed before a young couple. But they were available and moving out, and God used them mightily.

Are you truly available, so that the Holy Spirit has freedom to accomplish what He desires in and through your life? Then decide what God wants you to do, and step out in obedience!

When God Opens the Door

"When word came that all three had safely escaped, I was ecstatic but not surprised."

Vek Huong Taing, his wife, Samoeun, and their son, Wiphousana, arrive in southern California following their four-year ordeal in the jungles of Cambodia.

CHAPTER TEN

One Effectual, Fervent Prayer

It was a simple prayer, voiced by four men in Burma who loved the Lord and wanted Him to touch their nation in a wonderful way: "Lord, we ask You to send us a copy of the Four Spiritual Laws booklet."

The men had begun to meet regularly for prayer — for their Buddhist countrymen, as well as for themselves and for their own ministries. As they talked about how to best witness to others, they found that they needed a tool to help them share the gospel. One of the four had heard of a booklet called the Four Spiritual Laws which is used to tell others about Christ.

But he had no idea where to obtain a copy of the booklet, so the group began to pray, "Lord, send us a copy of the Four Spiritual Laws."

One evening, a deeply troubled young man called on one of the four gentlemen, who was a pastor. Someone had recommended that he contact a minister about all his problems. As they began to talk, the pastor inquired, "Have you ever heard about Jesus Christ?"

The young man replied, "Yes, a little," pulling a small booklet from his pocket. "Someone gave this to me recently. It's about Jesus."

Speechless, the pastor found himself staring at a copy of the Four Spiritual Laws! A merchant seaman whose ship was anchored in the Rangoon harbor had given it to the young Burmese man. Later that evening, the young man invited Christ into his life, and the pastor hastened to inform his three friends that God had, in a most extraordinary way, supplied the very booklet for which they had prayed...

* * *

This incident also marked the beginning of an answer to prayer for me. For three years I'd been trying to pray my way into Burma, but every time I would plan a trip, something always stopped it. Our ministry had no Christian contacts there, and we were eager to assist the Burmese church in some way.

Soon afterward I received a letter from Mr. O. Ang Tung, one member of the four-man prayer group in Rangoon. Explaining that he had just obtained the address of our ministry from the back of the Four Spiritual Laws booklet, Mr. Ang Tung requested more materials. He went on to ask if someone from our movement could come to Burma to teach the Christians how to use these materials.

At last, I had my contact in Burma! I immediately corresponded with Mr. Ang Tung, sharing that I would come to visit Burma soon. I explained the philosophy and strategy of our movement, and said that I'd be interested to meet any individuals he might feel were qualified to serve the Lord on our staff. Mr. Ang Tung replied in his next letter, "If I were only 50 years younger, I would like to be the first person to apply for your staff." Mr. Ang Tung was only 78 years old at the time!

When the time came for me to leave for my first visit to Burma, I was barraged with letters asking me to bring Bibles and other Christian literature with me. Bibles are permitted in Burma, but rarely are they available on the local market, and there are restrictions against bringing Burmese printed matter into the country.

Now, I've never considered myself a smuggler. Although God is blessing many groups who are secretly taking the Word of God into countries where it is prohibited, this is an area in which we as an organization have not been involved. Yet, with so many requests for Bibles, I knew I could not arrive in Rangoon empty-handed.

So without any experience in such an enterprise, I packed all the Burmese Bibles and Christian materials into one large suitcase which happened to have a combination lock. Evidently, I packed it so full of materials that when I closed it, one of the Bibles caught on the inside latch, depressed it and set a new combination on the lock. But I knew nothing about this — only that the bag weighed so much that my knees buckled when I tried to lift it!

As I flew to Burma, I prayed about the materials in my suitcase, reminding the Lord that these were His materials. "If You want them in Burma, Lord," I prayed, "then You will have to get them in somehow." I was not going to compromise my ethics to hedge on the truth, so I was eager to see what God would do. Unknown to me, He had already performed His miracle when I'd packed the suitcase at home!

As I entered the customs area, my heavy suitcase was placed on the counter and the customs inspector asked me to open it. The lock would not open. So I tried again. It still would not release. Over and over I tried, and finally the customs inspector spun the lock and tried his hand at the combination. Still it would not open.

As we worked over the combination, the inspector inquired why the suitcase was so heavy. I explained that it contained some books, glad that he never asked what kind of books!

Finally, the inspector exclaimed, "We will have to open this suitcase!" I told him I'd be happy for him to take a screwdriver and hammer to pry the lock open if he desired. Turning to me, he concluded, "That will not be necessary," and he cleared the suitcase. The materials were safely in the country!

Settled into my hotel, I assumed I'd have to pry the lock open myself. But first I put the suitcase on my bed, sat down beside it and prayed, "Lord, You've brought these materials into the country in Your own special way. I couldn't have done this. Now I ask You to open this suitcase."

I closed my eyes, spun the combination and pushed the latch ... and heard a soft click! The suitcase was open, and God had completed His miracle to make available many more precious Burmese Bibles for the local Christians.

Although that first experience will always be the most dramatic one in my memory, I've seen God perform similar miracles on every successive visit I've paid to Burma. Perhaps the most humorous time occurred several years later when Curt Mackey, area coordinator for Central Asia, and I went into Rangoon together.

This time our luggage was literally loaded with materials. We had scattered more than 300 Bibles and hundreds of copies of other literature all through the six pieces of luggage we had between us. I started through customs inspection first, opening my first suitcase. The inspector looked through my passport and papers and cleared the suitcase, which contained only English materials. Pleased, I closed the suitcase and it was set aside by a baggage boy.

As I went back to get another piece of luggage, Curt walked up with his first suitcase and handed the inspector his passport. The man looked at the suitcase and at Curt, and immediately he waved the luggage on through. Meanwhile, Curt went back to get another suitcase while I came up with my second bag and placed it before the inspector. He was examining someone else's luggage and simply glanced my way and said irritably, "That piece is cleared."

This same sequence happened three more times, as Curt and I cleared all six pieces of luggage without opening any but my first one! Each time the inspector became more irritated, and we became more confused. As we picked up our six pieces of luggage and left the customs inspection room, I asked Curt, "Do you have your passport?"

He gasped, "No!" So we left our luggage outside and returned to approach the inspector. Curt said, "You did not return my passport." He looked up and said, "Yes, I did." Then suddenly he saw the two of us standing side by side. Curt and I are the same age, the same height, of similar build and we both have blond hair that is turning grey. I'm sure that to a Burmese customs inspector, two blond-haired Americans — both wearing blue shirts that day! — must look very much alike.

He stood there with his mouth open, realizing the mistake he had made. As he returned Curt's passport with the completed customs forms, I'm sure he had no idea how many pieces of luggage he had cleared without inspecting. But we left rejoicing. God had confused that man so we could once again bring much-needed Bibles into Burma.

On each trip into Burma, I continued to pray and trust God to call out some Burmese Christians to become a part of our ministry. Soon God confirmed in my mind and in the mind of Matthew U Hla Win that he should join our staff. But when I accepted Matthew as our first Burmese staff member, I did not know how he could possibly leave Burma to attend our Manila training center.

In most Asian countries, travel is not that difficult. But for decades, it has been almost impossible for Burmese citizens to leave Burma, and when they do, it is a one-way ticket. Except for diplomatic reasons, a native Burmese citizen is almost never allowed to return once he has left the country. How was

Matthew, a government employee and father of eight children, ever going to overcome such an impossible obstacle? He had to tell the truth and yet somehow convince government authorities to permit him to spend six months in training for Christian work in the Philippines — and then return. We knew that God was able, and that it would take a miracle.

It was after one full year of praying and waiting that we received the long-awaited cable, stating that Matthew would be arriving in Manila to attend the Great Commission Training Center. Later we learned that Matthew was the first Christian in 12 years to be allowed to leave Burma for Christian purposes and then return home to be involved in Christian work!

Today, Matthew and our other Burmese staff who have since joined with him are conducting a revolutionary spiritual ministry on the university campuses and in the churches of Burma. In a significant way, their lives are helping to reach the isolated, staunchly Buddhist land of Burma for Christ.

Since that first Four Spiritual Laws booklet found its way to Rangoon, the Burmese translation has been printed in quantity. When I heard the following account from a recent student evangelistic meeting called College Life in Rangoon, I was reminded of the simple prayer of those four men which helped to bring it all about.

The crowd of more than 150 students grew silent as the young girl stood to speak. Her voice was soft and gentle, yet there was no mistaking the firm conviction with which she spoke.

"My name is Aye," she said, her tone hesitant at first. "I live in Paw Kan with my parents in a totally Buddhist community. I come from a strong Buddhist family, so my parents have always taught me about Buddhism.

"When I was about 16 years old, I knew of many sins in my life which were not known to my parents. These included stealing, fighting with my brothers and sisters and willful disobedience to my parents. I became more and more unhappy. I sought for peace through religious discipline, but I could find no peace.

"One day I heard a message from a Christian, and I understood that Jesus was calling out to all people who have worries and burdens, saying, 'Come unto Me, all you who are weary and heavy-laden, and I will give you rest.' When I heard this, I wanted to give all my burdens and worries to Christ, but I didn't know how.

"Later, one of my friends named Geoffrey came to me and shared a booklet called the Four Spiritual Laws. At that moment, I accepted Jesus Christ as my Savior and Lord. I became very happy and felt that all my burdens and worries were taken away. God gave me the real peace of mind for which I was searching.

"My life was totally changed. I became a happy, good and patient girl. Now I spend most of my time witnessing as a way of life, using the Four Spiritual Laws booklet. I love Jesus and will be faithful to Him until I die!"

Aye was barely seated when an older man walked briskly to the front of the crowd. Looking over the youthful faces, he spoke carefully:

"My name is U Saw Min. I am 55 years old. I am a Buddhist — not a so-called Buddhist, but a strong one. I have always been very interested in my Buddhism, and as Buddha taught, I try to do good works to be saved.

"I did not know much about Christianity. But one day my daughter, Aye Thida, came and told me that she received Jesus Christ as her Lord and Savior. I was very angry and sorry for what she had done. I told her not to change religions, because I would be ashamed among my religious friends. But she did not obey me, and she told me that Jesus Christ loves the whole world, and about what He has done for all humans. But I would not believe it.

"I tried to persuade her to change her mind, and sometimes I even threatened her. But she would not refuse Jesus. I began to wonder about her — how she had believed and how she had changed. I finally realized that something was making her different.

"One evening, three Christian friends who were guiding and teaching my daughter came to visit me unexpectedly. They brought the Bible and told me about Christ. We had a long discussion which lasted until 3 a.m.! At last I could not refuse what Jesus had done for my sins any longer. Buddha could not forgive my sins; but Jesus could. So I received Jesus Christ as my Lord and Savior.

"I became very happy. I was very sorry that I had spent 55

years of my life without knowing God's love and blessings, and without having fellowship with the Christians who are the children of God. Praise the Lord that I know Him now!"

Matthew U Hla Win tells me that Aye and her father have since led 18 other neighbors in their totally Buddhist community to Christ, and they are seeking assistance in forming a small church. All through God's loving faithfulness to a young teenage Buddhist girl!

Personal Application

Sometimes my prayers tend to put God into a box. In fact, very rarely are my prayers answered in the exact way I have actually pictured in my mind.

Four ordinary men in Burma recognized their need for a witnessing tool, and they asked God to supply it. They never dreamed that He would provide that booklet in such an unusual way, but they trusted Him to keep His promise to provide their needs:

> "And this is the confidence which we have before Him, that, if we ask anything according to His will, He hears us. And if we know that He hears us in whatever we ask, we know that we have the requests which we have asked from Him" (I John 5:14,15).

Have you asked God, in specific terms, to supply your needs? Perhaps you have some undefined areas of your life in which you want to see God work, but you have not actually prayed about them. I've learned that when I pray in faith, according to His will, with unselfish motives, when my heart attitude is right . . . God always answers my prayers! My part then is to watch and thank Him as He answers me, often in very unexpected ways.

When ordinary people pray, God moves in an extraordinary way. Your specific prayers can be the beginning of great things — in your own life, as well as in a much greater sphere of influence.

CHAPTER ELEVEN

Making an Eternal Difference

The question seems to come up often when I'm visiting with mutual friends in Birmingham, Ala.: "Do you really believe that ministering in small villages and tribes in such out-of-the-way places as Laos is the best investment of Bud and Elizabeth Newbold's time?"

I can understand why they ask. After all, Col. and Mrs. W. B. Newbold had an exceptional ministry for some 25 years in the southeastern part of the United States — leading Bible studies, teaching Bible classes over the radio, filling many speaking engagements. Their active ministry of spiritual multiplication literally touched thousands of lives all over Alabama and the Southeast.

And yet in 1972, the Newbolds set aside this fruitful ministry to travel around Southeast Asia and the Far East, training small handfuls of Asian believers in countries where advantages are not so plentiful. Both were 56 at the time — hardly the age to turn their backs on a comfortable home, to say nothing of small and dearly loved grandchildren, and start living out of a suitcase half the time on the other side of the world!

My reply to this question is always the same. I recount a conversation I had one day in Bangkok with the last American missionary to leave Laos as it fell to the Communists in 1975. As we discussed the future of Christianity in Laos, this gentleman commented. "You can be assured of one thing. There are small groups of Christians all up and down the country of Laos who are communicating their faith in Christ today because of the training they received from Mr. and Mrs. Newbold."

Think of it! Laotian believers under a Communist regime are telling others about Jesus today because one couple, now past 60 years of age, decided to put aside a glamorous ministry and to devote their lives to initiating spiritual multiplication where it is so desperately needed.

When the Newbolds first wrote to me, saying that God was calling them to invest the next chapter of their lives in Asia, I realized that, ultimately, their decision would touch the hearts of millions . . .

* * *

During our periodic visits to the United States, my wife and I are eager to share with everyone the mighty ways in which God is working across Asia, as well as the many needs we see for trained staff.

Because of our long-standing friendship with the Newbolds, whom we count as our spiritual parents, we always told them many of the exciting miracles God was doing. But since we knew of their fine ministry in the United States, it never occurred to us to challenge them to join us. However, sometime after one of our visits, Bud and Elizabeth Newbold sent word that God was calling them to Asia.

Later they related how, despite all the fulfilling avenues of spiritual ministry which they enjoyed in Birmingham, they began to sense a gentle nudging from the Lord in a new direction. They looked at our hometown of Birmingham: hundreds of Christians in the area were actively involved in sharing Christ and discipling others.

And then they looked at Asia: more than two-thirds of the world's entire population lives on this continent, now considered one of the most spiritually ripe areas of the world. The Christians are very few in number — often a negligible percentage — and without proper Christian training.

As the Newbolds considered these two realities, they could see only one alternative: to invest their lives in the area of greatest need and potential. Since they joined our staff team in Asia, they have multiplied themselves many times over in country after country by training Asian Christians to train others. Although they are far from their own families, God has blessed them with spiritual children and grandchildren from scores of nations and tribes across the Orient.

The Newbolds are just two of the powerful team of men and women whom God has called to serve Him through this movement in Asia. Each one has a fascinating story to share of God's calling, but none perhaps more unusual than the man God selected to fill the job of South Pacific coordinator, Hank Jones.

Seated on the roof of a home in Saigon, Vietnam, one day, I

watched from a bench as my host, Hank, barbecued our dinner. In the distance we could hear the constant "boom! boom!" of artillery shells exploding and bombs falling from airplanes. It was hardly a normal setting for a barbecue!

I watched Hank turn the steaks. After retiring from 20 years of active duty with the U.S. Marine Corps, Hank Jones had attended Bible college and seminary and then pastored a small, growing church in southern California.

Hank had told me that once a year he would deliver a missionary sermon to his congregation. To his knowledge, no one had ever responded to go to the mission field. But one particular Sunday morning, God spoke in a special way through Hank's annual missionary sermon — to Hank himself! A few months later, Hank and his wife were impressed to leave their pastorate and join the staff of Campus Crusade.

They moved their family to Saigon to serve as "missionaries" to the U.S. military personnel in South Vietnam. God used them in the lives of hundreds of U.S. soldiers, sailors and Marines serving in Vietnam. Within months of their arrival, Hank also helped found the Vietnam Campus Crusade for Christ ministry, and several Vietnamese joined our staff.

At that point the American forces were starting to withdraw from Vietnam. So while awaiting the steaks there on the rooftop, we discussed the future of our ministry in South Vietnam.

Finally, Hank turned from the charcoal broiler and said, "It appears to me that the objectives Marjorie and I had for our ministry here have been met. The Vietnamese ministry has been established, with trained staff who are able to train others, and the U.S. military ministry in Vietnam is now history. What do you have for me that could pose a greater challenge?"

I replied, "For many months, I have been praying for a person to launch and coordinate our ministry in Oceania and the South Pacific."

Quickly Hank responded, "I'll take the job!"

I was about to ask, "But, don't you want to pray about it?" when he explained.

"For 30 years I have been praying that God would give me the opportunity to go back and minister in the islands," he said, his eyes snapping with excitement. "As a Marine during World War II, I was assigned in the South Pacific. My job was a dangerous one, landing on many islands and cleaning up the snipers after victory over Japan."

He related that on island after island, he worked with islanders. "But at that time," he sighed, "all I had to offer the natives was soap, cigarettes and chocolate!" After the war, Hank and Marjorie came to know Christ as their Savior, and immediately they began praying for a chance to return to the islands — this time with something positive and lasting to offer, in the message of Jesus Christ.

Then I understood why Hank did not have to pray about my challenge. It was an answer to his prayers for the past 30 years!

In another unique way, God chose Curt Mackey to become our area coordinator for Central Asia and part of Southeast Asia. Curt had held many major responsibilities with our movement for more than 20 years. We had first had the privilege of working with Curt and Lois Mackey when I assumed my responsibilities in Asia. So after moving to the Orient, I had on several occasions challenged Curt, who had a strong interest in Asia, to join us. Yet it seemed that God met each one of my challenges with a more important responsibility for Curt in the United States at that time. It was becoming a wry ritual; every time I saw Curt, I challenged him to come to Asia. And each time he had to turn me down.

So when Elizabeth and I were flying to Seoul, Korea, for EXPLO '74, I announced, "This time when we see Curt and Lois, I'm not going to even bring up the subject of coming to Asia!" But God had a pleasant surprise for me, because within five minutes after we greeted each other, Curt volunteered that he was seriously considering my past challenges. He was interested in joining us within a year!

Curt's decision was more than a personal joy — it was an answer to my prayers. After serving as Central Asia coordinator for several years, Kundan Massey was about to vacate that position to become director of affairs for the Middle East. I was enthusiastic about Dr. Bright's appointment for Kundan, having recommended this leadership role for him. But we needed a replacement for him, and God confirmed that Curt Mackey was His choice. Within a matter of months, Curt

Making an Eternal Difference

was released from his numerous responsibilities in our U.S. ministry to join us with his family at our growing staff headquarters in the Philippines.

As you can see, God has provided a unique team of area coordinators to give leadership to our movement on the Asian continent. Col. Bud Newbold serves in the Far East and part of Southeast Asia; Curt Mackey serves in Central Asia and the remainder of Southeast Asia; and Hank Jones serves in Oceania and the South Pacific.

A diversified staff team has also been drawn together to lead our national staff teams across the continent. How I thank God every day for our staff leaders in the Orient — for their total availability to God, and for the privilege I have to serve the Lord Jesus Christ with them. Here is a sampling of the unique backgrounds of our national directors, who are some of the most dear men of God whom I have the opportunity to know:

ANANDA PERERA, a former devout Buddhist, directs Sri Lanka Campus Crusade.

EISUKE KANDA, whose uncle was one of the chief architects of the Pearl Harbor attack, now helps bring the peace of Christ as director of Japan Campus Crusade.

GEOFFREY FLETCHER, director of Australia Campus Crusade, was at one time director of evangelism for the world's largest Anglican diocese in Sydney, Australia.

ANDREW HO, the Hong Kong Campus Crusade director, escaped mainland China with his parents at the outset of the Communist takeover.

COL. RENERIO FUENTES, a survivor of the Bataan death march in World War II, directs Campus Crusade in the Philippines.

DAVID HOCK TEY, director of Malaysia Campus Crusade, has recruited almost all evangelical churches for a united outreach in that Muslim country.

DR. SOMDEE POOSAWTSEE, raised in an orphanage but now holding a Ph.D. in education administration, directs Thailand Campus Crusade.

AGUS LAY, a former university professor, leads Indonesia Campus Crusade.

ADON RONGONG directs Campus Crusade in Nepal,

where strong government and religious pressures persist.

STEPHEN SARKAR, a former university lecturer, directs Bangladesh Campus Crusade.

THE REV. Y. M. LAM directs Campus Crusade in the Portugese colony of Macau, considered the gambling capital of the Orient.

WES BRENNEMAN and WARREN WILLIS, two staff leaders from our U.S. Campus Ministry, now direct Campus Crusade in the Fiji Islands and Micronesia.

JOHN SELLMAN, a former engineering professor, leads the Campus Crusade ministry in New Zealand.

DO HUY HY, who escaped South Vietnam on one of the last flights out of Saigon, now directs a ministry with Vietnamese refugees in North America.

The list could go on and go on, describing the exceptional team of men with whom I serve. I have already mentioned elsewhere other valuable members of this team, such as Dr. Joon Gon Kim, director of Korea Campus Crusade; Thomas Abraham, director of India Campus Crusade; Victor Koh, director of Singapore Campus Crusade; Jonathan Chiu, director of Campus Crusade in Taiwan (Republic of China); Matthew U Hla Win, national representative of Burma Campus Crusade; and Vek Huong Taing, national representative of Cambodia Campus Crusade.

Space permits me to mention only a few of the men who play significant roles in this ministry, but I assure you that the wives who stand with all of these gentlemen are just as vital to our ministry. These ladies are also involved in their own strategic ministries. In addition to domestic responsibilities, they are involved in prayer ministry thrusts, discovery group Bible studies, village outreaches, medical clinics, high school ministries and evangelistic get-togethers for both Asian and Western women.

We also have a force of single women whom God has called to serve Him through our ministry in Asia. Shirley Mewhinney, who gave her life to serve the Lord as a missionary while in college, worked with me in the United States before we moved to Asia. She joined us in Singapore eight months later and has since become one of the backbones of the Asia-South Pacific headquarters. She has served as my secretary and as our publications director, and at the same time has maintained a vital personal ministry wherever we have been. Many Asian young ladies are on our staff today because of her life.

Gail Porter, who has been on Campus Crusade staff for 12 years, went to Korea to give secretarial assistance during EXPLO '74. While in Seoul for six months, God gave her a love for Asia. After EXPLO she transferred to our Asia-South Pacific headquarters in the Philippines to serve as secretary for our area coordinators.

Ann Bowman and Barbara Bolin serve as trainers at the Great Commission Training Center in Manila. The personal sacrifice that all these young ladies and a number of others like them are making to serve the Lord in another culture is recognized by very few. I will be eternally grateful to them for their ministries.

God brought a businessman formerly working with United Airlines to give leadership in administration and finances in our headquarters. When Sam and Joyce Newman sought God's will regarding my challenge to move their family of five children to the Philippines, Sam began to search the Scriptures. He states, "Suddenly I realized that Christ gave me the answer 2,000 years ago, when He gave the Great Commission!" It was so plain that he stopped searching, knowing that God wanted them in Asia. His assistant, Ed Neibling, first served on an *Agape* Movement team as an agricultural engineer when he came to Asia in 1974.

Operating ministries in 27 countries of Asia and the South Pacific requires almost every talent and skill imaginable. Obviously, this chapter can mention only a very few of the more than 700 staff members ministering across Asia. All of us consider ourselves nothing more than ordinary men and women who are, by God's grace and power, living extraordinary lives.

Personal Application

Some of the saddest words in the Bible are found in the last phrase of Ezekiel 22:30:

> "And I sought for a man among them, that should make up the hedge, and stand in the gap before Me for the land, that I should not destroy it; *but I found none*" (KJV).

Through the Scriptures we learn that God always looks for an individual when He has a job to be done — someone to be used by Him to build up the hedge — a person who has something positive to offer. He seeks out someone who is willing to stand in the gap, not merely sit in the pew!

The need is undeniable; the secret is our willingness. Are you willing, even as a graying Col. Newbold was, to stand in the gap for God? Saying "yes" to God today may make an eternal difference for an entire tribe or nation of people, for all for whom Christ died.

CHAPTER TWELVE

Vast Work of the Spirit

Sitting in the student center at the American University in Beirut, Lebanon, I began to talk with an Arab student about spiritual matters. As a Palestinian Muslim, this student assumed that most Americans are Christians and support Israel. He was against both, and he began to express his feelings very loudly. In fact, he was yelling angrily, so that almost every person in that section of the student center turned around to stare at us.

Calling me an American imperialist, he accused me of being interested only in forcing my politics and religion on poor, unsuspecting people. Then, in a loud tone, he launched into a five-minute dissertation on his evaluation of the American political situation as it related to the Middle East.

Finally, when he paused for a breath, I told him, "I have not come to talk about politics." I said that I agreed with some things he'd said about my country's political stand, and naturally I disagreed with others. Furthermore, I related, "I have not come here to talk about religion. Instead, I'm here to explain how you can have a direct, personal relationship with God through Jesus Christ."

For the next 30 minutes, we talked about the person of Jesus Christ. Never have I seen such a radical transformation in a person within a few moments. At one point, he was yelling at me with hatred in his eyes. Thirty minutes later he sat enraptured with the thought of how much Jesus Christ loved him as an individual. After a few more minutes, he invited Christ to come into his life. An hour earlier, he had considered me an arch enemy — but now we were brothers in Christ!

I asked this Palestinian student, "Have you ever been to church before?" He replied, "I have never been inside a church. All I know about Jesus is what my religion has taught me." Yet the first time he heard the truth, this student responded to Jesus, because the Spirit of God was at work in his heart . . .

* * *

I see this scene being repeated time and time again here in

Asia. I am convinced that millions of people are hungry to know God, because everywhere I go, individuals readily respond when they hear the truths of God's love and forgiveness made known in Christ. I can see this search for truth when I'm riding in modern comfort through the Orient's large, cosmopolitan cities such as Tokyo, Osaka, Hong Kong and Singapore. And it's just as visible when I'm walking through the continent's never-ending rural villages, where the pages of history are turned back hundreds of years.

Asia is home for 60% of the world's people. Only *one percent* of these are Christians. The majority are Hindus, Muslims, Buddhists and Animists.

But Asians seem to be tired of "religion" these days. What a paradox — on the very continent where Eastern religions and cults (now so popular in "Christian" America!) were born, great numbers of Asians are open and even eager to learn about the claims of Jesus Christ. I believe that the response to the gospel in Asia today is unprecedented in human history.

Probably no group in Asia observes the truth of this hunger more regularly than the Crossroads, a cross-cultural music team traveling across the Orient with Campus Crusade. In the last six years, this musical group, directed by Leon Obien, has performed live before audiences totalling more than half a million people across Asia.

The setting could be Stadium Negara in Kuala Lumpur, Malaysia, before a crowd of 8,000 students . . . or a bamboo stage in front of 2,000 villagers in rural, humid Indonesia . . . or before 100 guests in Nagoya, Japan, including the governor of the prefecture and his staff . . . or on national television in Taiwan (Republic of China), exposing the bulk of the national population to the gospel . . . or making history in Bangkok, Thailand, by presenting Christ for the first time in the National Theater . . . or at EXPLO '74 in Seoul, Korea, singing in Korean before more than a million people.

Wherever the Crossroads have gone, people listen and respond. Despite the fact that audiences are predominantly Hindu, Buddhist, Animist or Islamic, at least 45,000 people have invited Jesus Christ into their lives during the Crossroads performances.

But rather than citing a whole chapter of facts and figures to confirm the unique openness in Asia to the gospel of Christ,

"Great numbers of Asians are open and even eager to learn about the claims of Jesus Christ."

Three young Vietnamese watch with interest as a Christian communicates the Four Spiritual Laws. This photo portrays the spiritual hunger that swept Vietnam prior to the communist takeover in 1975.

I have chosen to relate what is happening in the lives of ordinary Asian men and women — in our big cities, in villages, on high school and college campuses, on islands — wherever the truth about Jesus Christ is being proclaimed. Many of these individuals I have met firsthand; others I have met only through the reports and visits I receive from our Asian staff.

These incidents are gathered from the entire Asia-South Pacific area of affairs, which falls naturally into four geographic regions: the Far East, Southeast Asia, Central Asia and the South Pacific.

As you read of the miraculous turn of events we are seeing in nearly every nation of Asia, multiply the ministry of Campus Crusade by the scores of other evangelical groups operating effectively across the Orient — and then perhaps you will begin to believe as I do: The Great Commission can and will be fulfilled in Asia by 1980! I do not dare to say this from a human perspective, but the reality of reaching Asia by 1980 becomes more and more plausible as we witness the miraculous moving of God's Spirit today.

The Far East

Economic affluence characterizes the Far East region more than any other part of Asia. Buddhism remains the traditional religion of these nations — Korea, Japan, Taiwan (Republic of China), Hong Kong, Macau and the Peoples' Republic of China — but because of their rapid economic growth, money has become the real idol. Consequently, this development has created a spiritual hunger which never before existed.

JAPAN for years has deserved the reputation of being a spiritual desert. Percentage-wise there are more educated pastors speaking to fewer people on Sunday morning in Japan than in any other country of the world. But today in the churches of Japan, God's people are turning to repentance and prayer, and God has begun to heal their land.

When our staff first proposed Here's Life, Okinawa, the Japanese pastors were very skeptical, thinking that such a strategy would never work in Japan. But after some of them visited Here's Life, Hong Kong, they returned with a concrete vision. Through use of mediated training, 57 of the 63

Vast Work of the Spirit

churches in Okinawa trained their laymen — some churches reported as many as seven trainings! Some 460 prayer groups formed to pray for the media campaign.

Before Here's Life, Okinawa, average church attendance in all 63 churches was 1,842. But look at the figures that resulted from the media campaign:

People who received Christ before media campaign	431
People who responded to the media campaign	10,806
Number of people contacted personally	3,434
Number of people who heard the gospel personally	2,061
Number who indicated they received Christ	1,147
Number who enrolled in follow-up Bible studies	597

Two very significant factors emerge from these statistics: First, in a country considered a spiritual desert, more than one out of every two people who heard the gospel responded to receive Christ! And second, the number of Christians in Okinawa increased by 85% through the Here's Life movement!

KOREA stands out to me as a remarkable example of the spiritual harvest which a praying church can expect. Today, Christian publications regularly report the phenomenal results of several decades of prayer, including the significant role which EXPLO '74 played.

Several years after EXPLO '74, I participated in a Leadership Training Institute in Korea where students were challenged to spend two weeks sharing their faith in Christ throughout the 59,000 villages of South Korea. Some 1,800 students volunteered, taking specific assignments to share Christ with village leaders in defined geographic areas. They were to live by faith with whatever money they had, trusting God to supply their needs.

The results were staggering. Of the 165,250 villagers who heard how to know Christ personally, 123,560 indicated that they had received Jesus Christ by faith! And thousands upon thousands of these were village leaders.

TAIWAN (REPUBLIC OF CHINA) provides an excellent example of what can happen in a nation, almost overnight, when a well-known leader boldly speaks out for Christ. In April of 1975, Generalisimo Chiang Kai-shek, the former President, went to be with the Lord. Although he was known to be a Christian, he surprised everyone by speaking boldly of his personal love for the Lord Jesus Christ in his last will and testament, left to the Chinese people.

God used this to create an awareness of God as never before. Our own ministry statistics changed radically after his death. The number of decisions for Christ doubled. Nationally, the sale of Bibles increased greatly. Church attendance grew. Because public school students were required to memorize Chiang Kai-shek's will, teachers wrote: "Our students are asking us, 'Who is this Jesus Christ, whom Chiang Kai-shek followed?'" Spiritually, a new day has dawned in Taiwan!

HONG KONG and MACAU stand as gateways to the Chinese mainland. So what takes place in these relatively small colonies can have a significant spiritual impact upon the world. Every day, despite strong Communist opposition in some areas, more Christians in these cities are accepting their responsibility to win and disciple others. One high school discipleship program in Macau, for example, involves 20 students. Each afternoon they spend 30 minutes in door-to-door witnessing with our staff. This vital half-hour each day, arranged by individual schedule, helps maintain their level of commitment, which is frequently challenged by leftist persecution.

Southeast Asia

For four decades, most nations in Southeast Asia have lived with war or the threat of war. Much of World War II was fought across Southeast Asia. After World War II ended, war did not end — only the enemy changed, but the battleground remained the same.

People who live under the constant threat of imminent violence are extremely open to spiritual truths. The peoples of Vietnam, Cambodia, Laos, Thailand, Malaysia, Singapore, Indonesia and the Philippines are no exception.

THE PHILIPPINES experiences a stronger Christian heritage than any other country of the Orient because of the influence of the Roman Catholic Church, which came to this nation 400 years ago. However, like many countries of a similar background, religion has been reduced to a code of ethics. So when reality in knowing Jesus Christ personally is offered, the response is phenomenal both on the university campus and in the lay community.

One nation-wide Leadership Training Institute which we conducted at the University of the Philippines in Quezon City was endorsed by the Philippine Secretary of Education. Approximately 1,000 students representing at least 60 colleges and universities from all over the Philippine Islands gathered for five days of intensive training in evangelism.

"Vision 80," the conference theme, challenged students to visualize all of the Philippine Islands exposed to the claims of Christ by 1980. After I had shared a message on the Great Commission the closing night, 300 of the students, graduates and faculty members present walked to the front of the auditorium to indicate they were committing the rest of their lives to help saturate the Philippines with the claims of Christ. What a privilege to send them forth with our Lord's promise, "Lo, I am with you always, even to the end of the age."

After the LTI, one student could hardly wait to share her faith with fellow students in her dorm. Within weeks, she had formed a Bible study that included 30 new Christians!

VIETNAM and its people have been receptive to the gospel throughout the recent tragic years of that nation. Just before Saigon fell, while it was being surrounded by Communist troops, students continued to be anxious to hear about Christ. Our staff had begun evangelistic student meetings called College Life to help reach these students a few months earlier. I have learned that just two days before the final defeat and collapse of Saigon, when chaos and confusion reigned throughout the city, more than 200 students gathered at a College Life meeting to hear how they could know Christ personally. With a Communist takeover and probable persecution for Christian beliefs expected within days, students still had a strong desire to know and follow Jesus Christ!

THAILAND is a staunchly Buddhist land living under the constant threat of Communist takeover. And yet in every area of society, the Thai people are responding to the gospel as never before. Recently, during the Here's Life, Bangkok campaign, more than 7,000 letters were received, mostly from Thai Buddhists, expressing the hunger that existed in their lives.

One story in particular touched my heart. A young Thai girl who was a Buddhist was climbing out of the window of her Bangkok apartment to jump and commit suicide. As she looked down at the street, she saw the poster reading, "I Found It! You Can Find It Too . . . New Life in Jesus Christ!" Seeing the telephone number on the poster, she climbed back in and made a call, expressing her desperation. A campaign worker immediately went to call on her, and this desperate young lady found the answer to the problems plaguing her as she opened her life to the Lord Jesus Christ.

MALAYSIA offers a tremendous spiritual challenge as a mixed country, both racially and religiously. Nearly 50% of the population is Malays, a majority of whom are Muslims. The laws of the land make it very difficult to share the gospel with Malays. However, the remaining half of the people are mostly Chinese, along with a small percentage of Indian and other nationalities, and the doors are open to minister among them today.

One of the most remarkable young men I've met in a long time is a Chinese high school student in Malaysia. If everyone who took our training caught the vision this young man has, the world would be turned upside down for Jesus very quickly! Several years ago he was among 30 students from his school who attended a Leadership Training Institute where students were challenged to win their schools for Christ. They went home and started witnessing, and within two weeks 15 students had trusted Christ. They continued to witness boldly, and the next year 60 students attended the high school LTI.

When this young man came up with an Every Student Plan to present the claims of Jesus personally to every non-Malay student, other Christian students in the city became so interested that he set up a series of training classes for 120 students. Within three years, more than 90% of the non-Malay students in that city had been personally exposed to the gospel!

"We believe that high schools are strategic in the total ministry of God," this young man told me. "About 2.5 million Malaysians, or one-fourth of the population, are students."

SINGAPORE is another multi-racial society. On this island, the bulk of the population lives in government-built, high-rise housing estates. A Campus Crusade staff family ministering at one of these housing estates has seen 2,030 of the 4,600 residents whom they have exposed to the gospel indicate decisions for Christ! Presently 150 men, women and students meet in their small discipleship groups each week, scheduled one after another all Saturday afternoon and evening.

I remember when one staff girl in Singapore was given three new staff trainees and asked to launch a ministry at National Chung Hsing University. God so worked through their lives that in less than five months so many of the girls in the dorms had heard the claims of Christ that it was difficult to find anyone who hadn't heard of the Four Spiritual Laws already! So this staff girl and her team began witnessing at the boarding houses off campus.

INDONESIA, a Muslim country, has many areas where no churches or active Christian witness exist. Such was the case of the village of Barukan in Salatiga, until a staff member of Indonesia Campus Crusade shared Christ with Mr. Subakir, a village teacher, and his wife. After this couple received Christ, they led a number of their relatives to the Lord, and soon neighbors all over the village were hearing about Christ. The staff returned to conduct a Lay Institute for Evangelism, and the multiplication process continued. There are now 300 believers in Barukan, and their new church, affiliated with a local denomination, has already begun an outreach in a nearby area where 60 new converts are meeting for prayer and Bible study!

Central Asia

On the map, Central Asia appears small and insignificant so far as land mass is concerned. But it is the most densely populated area of the world, and more people starve to death there every day than in any other area. Political turmoil seems to be a way of life there, and in matters of religion, 99% of the people profess Buddhism, Hinduism or Islam. Yet God is at work, setting millions free from man-made religions in India, Sri Lanka, Bangladesh, Burma, Nepal, Bhutan and Tibet.

INDIA represents 17% of the world's population. Because an overwhelming majority of these people are scattered throughout the nation's villages, Campus Crusade has been helping train village evangelists, many of whom have had little training in personal evangelism. In the state of Kerala, hundreds of thousands have heard the gospel through village evangelists. One evangelist shared this incident:

"My experiences in helping to evangelize my hometown were rich and varied. Once as I entered a home, I found an alcoholic living there, I didn't know whether I should leave the house or should speak to this man. At last I decided to share Christ with him. When I came to the two circles which indicate two different types of lives, he started crying and shared with me how disgusted he was with the kind of life he was leading. As I assured him that no matter what kind of life he was leading, Jesus wanted to come into his life and change it, he fell to his knees and prayed with me to invite Christ into his heart."

BANGLADESH, another Muslim country, has weathered a number of recent disasters, including earthquakes, severe tidal wave damage, the terrors of war and serious famine. Only Christ can meet man's needs at times like these. In the city of Dacca, Campus Crusade staff are hosting Human Life, an evangelistic gathering of students and lay people. As many as 300 people crowd into the meeting room at one time to hear about Jesus Christ. A report came across my desk that 150 people indicated on comment cards after a Human Life meeting that they had invited Christ into their lives. They represented Christian, Muslim and Hindu backgrounds.

BURMA is remembered as the land where the famous missionary Adoniram Judson labored for 14 years before he saw the first Buddhist convert. Today, the seeds sown by Mr. Judson and others like him are coming into full bloom.

A few months ago Burma Campus Crusade began to conduct some open-air evangelistic meetings in Rangoon. Everyone assured our staff no one would come, but they went ahead with their plans. Their system of promotion was very simple: they sat some speakers atop one truck and then passed out handbills around the city, inviting people to hear about "New Life in Jesus Christ." That evening, more than 10,000 people crowded up to hear the gospel proclaimed! At the conclusion of the meeting, those who wanted to receive Jesus Christ were invited to pray silently. But as the speaker began the prayer, a phrase at a time, he was astonished to hear a great roar of voices repeating it after him! Literally hundreds of Burmese Buddhists came into the kingdom of our Savior that night.

SRI LANKA is no different. I was thrilled when I read in a letter that one of the more well-known movie stars in Sri Lanka persuaded producers to postpone the shooting of her current film for one week so that she could attend a Lay Institute for Evangelism! The actress was recognized and stopped by people all over the town where she and other LIFE conferees were witnessing for Christ. When she stopped by the local police station, this lady led the Buddhist officer-in-charge to Christ and then challenged him, "You should have this message communicated to all your staff!" He agreed, and a few days later he invited a Campus Crusade staff member to present Christ to his entire police force.

NEPAL faces many religious and political hindrances to sharing the message of Christ. In spite of this, earnest Christians in this isolated, "closed" country are being trained to share their faith. At one institute for 69 conferees, the participants exposed 108 people to the claims of Christ. Since any organized, public effort of evangelism would not be permitted, they shared Christ with their relatives and neighbors during the witnessing session. They saw 41 indicate they had received Christ as Savior!

The South Pacific

Compared to the rest of the world, the South Pacific presents an entirely unique challenge to evangelism. The relatively few number of people living there are scattered on small islands covering millions of square miles of ocean, extending all the way "down under" to Australia and New Zealand. Our strategy throughout these sparsely-populated islands has been to establish a central ministry which reaches out to the surrounding areas.

THE TRUK ISLANDS hosted Micronesia's first barefoot Pastors' Institute for Evangelism on the island of Tol. Twenty-five pastors sailed to this tiny island for the five-day institute, where they were expected to go out and share their faith in Christ one day. The director of the sponsoring mission shook his head, saying, "It will never happen! These pastors have never gone out witnessing, and it is against their custom to do so."

However, staff conducting the training challenged the pastors to "conduct an experiment to find out if Truk is the only place in the world where this method of sharing the gospel will not work." The pastors responded, and 42 of the 127 adults with whom they shared invited Christ into their lives! The church district president was totally convinced of the method when a man to whom he witnessed turned over his implements of witchcraft, renounced the devil and prayed to receive Christ by faith.

FIJI is one of several islands where whole villages have been transformed soon after the gospel reached them. In a small remote village in Fiji, more than 800 indicated decisions for Christ during a weekend of meetings conducted by our staff. One year later, when a staff member returned to the village, more than 400 people were regularly attending church and participating in small group Bible studies.

AUSTRALIA has great potential for the cause of Christ, particularly as churches labor together. When students in the Sydney area were challenged to volunteer their time during semester break to assist in strengthening the outreach of seven churches, more than 70 Campus Crusade students responded. During the week-long project, more than 2,200 people were confronted with the claims of Christ. This was a radical approach for many of these churches.

NEW ZEALAND is a similar nation where people seem to "play at church" until they meet Christ personally. Then a new life begins! When a pastor in New Plymouth became obedient to God's command to make disciples, he had his congregation trained to share their faith. One night the pastor and one of his laymen knocked at the door of a neighborhood home. The pastor shared the Four Spiritual Laws booklet with the couple, who both committed their lives to Christ. The husband shared his testimony at the next morning church service:

"Before becoming a Christian, I saw God as a small light at the end of a long tunnel. I kept putting obstacles in front of that light. When the pastor confronted me with the Four Spiritual Laws, the obstacles were completely gone, and I was at the light. All this happened just because two people knocked on our door. I think thousands of people in New Plymouth are waiting for someone to knock on their door!"

A few weeks later, this church received 17 new members by profession of faith, including 14 won to Christ in their own homes through these visitation teams.

In various countries of Asia, we have specialized teams representing The *Agape* Movement of Campus Crusade. Doctors, nurses, teachers and other professionals practice their respective specialties while presenting the gospel to those with whom they come in contact.

Some time ago, a medical team with Campus Crusade's *Agape* Movement began to minister one day a week in Barrio (Village) Pinget, a remote mountain village. In this barrio live 180 families, all Bontoc natives. Many follow animistic beliefs, and some are involved in witchcraft. But God began to work in their lives. So many villagers came to Christ through the *Agape* team's first two months of ministry that the barrio council met and passed a resolution to change their name to "Easter Barrio." This new name was to signify the new life they had found in Jesus Christ.

These are stories about ordinary people, but it is my hope that they have given you a tiny glimpse of the breadth of what our God is doing through thousands of people in Asia today. It is obvious that there is no lack of hunger for God in these countries. In actuality, the major obstacle preventing many millions from coming to Christ is simply that not enough Christians are going to the people!

When God's children are obedient, and they go in response to His command, then miracles such as you have just read about begin to happen.

Personal Application

Let me remind you of that passage in Matthew 28:18-20 which we call the Great Commission of our Lord Jesus Christ to His Church:

> "I have been given all authority in heaven and earth. Therefore go and make disciples in all the nations, baptizing them into the name of the Father and of the Son and of the Holy Spirit, and then teach these new disciples to obey all the commands I have given you; and be sure of this — that I am with you always, even to the end of the world" (LB).

We need to recognize that the hour is late; God has prepared the hearts of people all around us, and He who has all authority has commanded us to "go." As His children, we have a responsibility to obey God, based on our love and appreciation for Him. God's responsibility is to prepare hearts and work in lives as we go.

This mandate we have does not begin tomorrow — it begins today. Don't put off obeying God — "go" as He told you, whether it be next door or clear around the world.

CHAPTER THIRTEEN

A Spiritual Epidemic

Telephones were ringing frantically all over the room — 25 green phones and 15 red ones. Surrounded by the busy din, smiling Chinese and Indian telephone operators picked up their instruments and began to respond to the callers.

The operators often nodded vigorously — listening, explaining, sometimes noting down addresses and phone numbers.

I watched in fascination, caught up in the flurry of activity. It was explained to me that the telephone instruments were color coded. Those who spoke Chinese dialed a number that connected them with a red phone, and a Chinese-speaking operator would answer. Those who spoke English dialed another number to a green phone manned by an English-speaking operator.

My heart beat with excitement, for I was standing in the Central Telephone Center for Here's Life, Singapore. Seven and a half years before, my family and I had moved to Singapore, to begin in that great city our adventure of living and ministering in the Orient. Now this entire city was being confronted with the gospel in a few weeks' time!

The busy telephone operators were picking up their phones to begin conversations, "I found it! Are you interested in finding new life in Jesus Christ?"

Inquirers who responded positively had their addresses recorded, and then these contacts were passed on immediately to trained Christians from local churches in their community. These Christians, all volunteers for the special evangelistic effort, went out to contact the individuals personally, sharing a booklet, "Here's How You Can Find It Too!"

I shook my head in amazement and thanksgiving to see what God was doing in Singapore through the Here's Life movement. Before it was over, surveys would indicate that 80% of the city's 2.2 million people were made aware that new life could be found in Jesus Christ! A total of 68,513 people would respond to the 10 different types of media repeating the invitation, "I found it! You can find it, too."

The plan was incredibly simple — and it was being carried out by a comparative handful of Christians — and yet it was starting to spread like an epidemic into every major city of Asia ...

* * *

Here's Life, Asia had its origin in the midst of most unusual circumstances. In April, 1975, the Republic of South Vietnam, Cambodia and Laos fell to the Communists, causing a cloud of spiritual depression all across the Orient. For several days, I personally was very depressed as I tried to understand these events, and as I thought of my many friends who had suddenly become isolated inside these countries. I was unable to reconcile the tragedy taking place with our projected goal of helping reach Asia and the world with the gospel by 1980. So I began to question, "Why, God?"

But after four days of unbelief, I finally decided once again to trust God — and praise Him rather than question Him. Almost immediately after I started thanking Him for what He was going to do, the Lord gave me the assurance that the fall of Vietnam, Cambodia and Laos would be the motivation needed in so many countries to stir the church into action. God was going to use a depressing situation to stimulate Christians to get involved in the fulfillment of the Great Commission in their nations before it was too late.

Today, I do not know what will happen in Vietnam, Cambodia and Laos — but I do trust in the sovereignty of God. The Great Commission is not man's idea — it is God's idea. In God's own sovereign way, He will provide ways and means to reach the people of these three countries with the gospel.

Out of this despair, which for me was transformed into a time of faith and thanksgiving when I chose to trust the Lord, was born the idea of Here's Life, Asia.

After the fall of Indochina, the urgency of the hour was very apparent to me, as well as to many other earnest Christians in the Orient. Many surrounding countries were in great danger, along with nations in other parts of Asia. "The spreading of the gospel must be accelerated!" ran through my mind like a theme song, and I was plagued continually by

A Spiritual Epidemic

questions: "How could this be done? What could we as a movement do?" And then God revealed His plan.

Here's Life, America had just been developed and implemented in the first American city. When I heard of this city saturation concept, my immediate reaction was negative. "It'll never work in Asia!" I thought. But again I had to face my unbelief. I hadn't even investigated the strategy, much less given it a fair chance to work! So I decided to go and learn all I could about it.

It was while I was attending a Here's Life strategy conference in the United States that God began to show me that this plan was an answer to years of prayer on the part of Christians all over the world. Through Here's Life, the ministry of churches across the Orient could be accelerated, and millions of people could be confronted with the claims of Jesus Christ in a very short period of time. I was getting excited!

One of the major barriers in saturating most countries of the Orient with the gospel was the fact that relatively few Christians live here. Often, Christians hardly make up one percent of an entire national population. For example, Japan is the sixth largest country in the world, but the Christian population there is less than one-half of one percent!

Never before had Christians in Asia come up with an answer for the perennial questions: "How can so many people be confronted with the claims of Jesus Christ by so few Christians? How can Jesus Christ become a relevant issue in such a society?"

But when I looked at the Here's Life strategy, I realized that God was showing us how a very small number of Christians could expose cities of millions of people to the gospel, giving them the opportunity to express a desire to receive Christ.

A major strength of Here's Life, I realized, lay in the fact that it centers in the local church. Very simply, we are helping to get together two groups of people: The people who already know Jesus Christ personally, with the people who would *like* to know Him! So the purpose of Here's Life is to train Christians in the local church in personal evangelism and discipleship, and then to place them in contact with those who've expressed a desire to know more about a personal relationship with Jesus Christ.

In order to create widespread awareness that new life can be found in Jesus Christ, many forms of mass media are used to blanket an entire city with the phrase, "I found it!" During the first "suspense week," newspapers, billboards, posters, radio, television and even buttons appear all over the city proclaiming, "I found it!" In the cities of Asia where Here's Life has been conducted so far, public surveys have determined that an average of at least 70% of the total population in these cities was made aware that "I found it!" referred to new life in Jesus Christ!

With the curiosity of the city aroused, the "reveal" portion of the media campaign declares, "I found it! You can find it, too . . . new life in Jesus Christ." During the reveal phase, the public is invited to respond by telephone, drop-box coupons or mail-in forms to request information on how they can find this new life in Jesus Christ. In this manner millions are exposed, and the thousands who respond are contacted personally by trained campaign workers.

Of course, the most vital aspect of each Here's Life campaign is not the media campaign but rather the evangelistic training conducted in the individual churches. Through this, Christian laymen and students are prepared to lead others to Christ and then help them grow in their new life to become strong disciples. Over half of all those who have indicated decisions for Christ through Here's Life campaigns in Asia have enrolled in a follow-up Bible study series. Conducted by the local churches, these classes form a natural step toward active Christian involvement and church membership.

As I had expected, there was a certain amount of skepticism among church leaders when we began to introduce the Here's Life strategy in various cities across Asia. However, God had used EXPLO '74 in many of their lives as a hint of what He really wanted to do in the way of miracles across the Orient. With the doors of many countries closing and a fresh realization of the urgency of the hour, Here's Life put before them a solid, concrete plan of evangelism and spiritual multiplication centered in the churches.

God blessed and multiplied beyond our greatest hope. Within two years of the inception of Here's Life, Asia, successful campaigns had been conducted in 25 major cities of the Orient — Manila and Baguio in the Philippines, the city of

A Spiritual Epidemic

Singapore, Malaysia's seven largest cities and 15 cities in Taiwan (Republic of China).

A commitment to prayer became the real secret of the success of the Here's Life movement. The personal time involvement of thousands of campaign workers was focused first of all on prayer.

Before Here's Life, Manila, more than 2,000 persons signed up for 15-minute segments of prayer time on 24-hour prayer chains across the city. At least 15,000 people gathered in the city's Araneta Coliseum for a day-long prayer rally before the media campaign was launched.

In Singapore, at least 8,000 Christians were involved in the prayer chains. When one "prayer warrior," a woman in Singapore, heard about the 24-hour prayer chains, she immediately signed up as a team leader. A few days later, while still in the process of enlisting prayer members for her team, this lady personally got up three times each night to pray for 15 minutes — at 12:15 a.m., 2:15 a.m. and 4:15 a.m.!

On Singapore's Labor Day, 400 Christians from both Chinese- and English-speaking churches united together for all-night prayer. It was that night, the Here's Life staff told me later, when so many Singapore Christians first caught the vision that national saturation of Singapore with the gospel was possible!

For the first two months before the campaign in Manila, I was in and out of the city on a weekly basis. Then during the campaign I talked with pastors and lay leaders who were involved, and went on some home calls myself. During the "reveal" week, I hosted a number of our national directors who came to observe the potential of Here's Life in their own countries.

What a rewarding experience for all of us! Within two weeks, 23,000 telephone calls came into the Manila telephone center, and over 75% of these callers gave a positive answer to the question: "If you could find new life in Jesus Christ, you would like to, wouldn't you?"

A similar process was used with 800 response boxes strategically placed city-wide. Each participating church was assigned several boxes to distribute and operate in its assigned neighborhood. Citizens were invited to fill in a coupon and drop it in the box if they were interested in "finding it." In just one 20-minute test-run conducted during "suspense" week, 260 cards were dropped into one box.

During a three-week period in Manila and Baguio, Here's Life received 209,830 media responses! Typical of many other Asian cities, where masses are eager to know God personally and the trained Christians are so few, both of these cities posed the pleasantly frustrating problem of having more inquiries than could possibly be followed up during the campaign.

Even so, more than 1,900 campaign workers were able to contact 15,894 of those making inquiries before the media campaign ended. Of these, 87% listened to a complete presentation of the gospel, and 9,242 indicated they had found new life in Christ. Over half of these new believers expressed a desire to join a neighborhood Bible study.

Church leaders were enthusiastic over the results. Prior to Here's Life, Capital City Alliance Church had only one Sunday school service. Now, Pastor Valmike Apuzen reports they have three morning services, two Sunday schools and three congregations meeting outside their church!

The city coordinator for Here's Life, Manila shared a remarkable story with me. About three weeks before the Praise and Prayer Rally planned for Here's Life, Manila, some 20 Manila pastors gathered to share what God had been doing in their churches through the "I found it!" campaign. The pastor of the Church of the Holy Redeemer, the Rev. Santiago C. Luzares of the United Church of Christ in the Philippines, told the group, commenting on II Timothy 2:2:

"This verse says we should train others to teach also, and this is exactly what I have been doing in my church. Even if I am no longer the pastor in the Church of the Holy Redeemer, the work will go on, the church will go on, the training will go on — *even without me!*"

Only 22 days later, Pastor Luzares went to be with the Lord. The week before he had a fatal motor accident near his church in Quezon City, Pastor Luzares prepared a testimony for the Praise and Prayer Rally. He said, in part:

"I have seen some firsts in the life of the Church of the Redeemer in Project 6, Quezon City. Our church has reached more people for the Lord in six months than in all her previous 18 years put together. Over 500 people were personally given the opportunity to say 'Yes' or 'No' to Jesus through the Four

A Spiritual Epidemic

Spiritual Laws booklet. Any Christian who can read can be enlisted. For the first time, the church has had campaign workers go out regularly and in an organized manner. The church is seeing her Jerusalem reached."

And then he concluded his testimony by writing, "The most important task of a shepherd (pastor) is to train his people to share the gospel ... this is the meaning of the concept called spiritual multiplication."

Four months after the campaign, the Rev. Fred B. de Leon reported that his church had recorded a record number of baptisms. "The yearly average of baptisms was 10," he wrote. "But as of June this year, we have already 47 souls attributed to the Here's Life program and a record of not less than 150 professions of faith by personal soul-winning." He also reported 12 new home Bible study groups, averaging 14 people per group, organized in the church.

In Singapore, the Here's Life movement was under the leadership of 28-year-old Victor Koh, director of Singapore Campus Crusade for Christ. Most of Singapore's leading pastors are mature, grey-headed gentlemen, and in the Chinese culture one's age is very significant. And yet these Christian leaders were being trained and taking direction from this young man who would not normally be considered qualified to administer any advice. God had overcome these natural barriers because He had in His hands a young man who desired to be used mightily by Him.

Victor became involved in our ministry while a second-year student at the University of Singapore. At that time, Victor knew God wanted him in full-time Christian service. His only question was, "In what position can I have the most profound impact for Christ upon my country?"

During that time, the three of us in Singapore (Elizabeth and myself and my secretary, Shirley) had been praying for national staff, asking God to impress various individuals to join our ministry. During a three-day retreat which we planned for 12 students, God confirmed His call to nine of those students, one of whom was Victor Koh. Following graduation, he and several other young students joined staff, received their training and began ministries of aggressive evangelism and discipleship in Singapore.

As a result, the campus ministries in Singapore expanded.

However, because all of the staff were so young, many pastors hesitated to allow them to teach and train in their churches. Patiently and lovingly, Victor and his staff got involved in churches at every opportunity. Soon they were invited to train young people in the church youth departments and Sunday schools.

Before long, pastors began to recognize something unusual: Their young people were sharing Christ as a way of life, and they were bringing their converts back into the churches! The ice was breaking, and pastors began to invite these youthful staff members to train their laymen.

When our staff team shared the vision of Here's Life, Singapore at a special pastors' breakfast sometime later, the response was immediate. Pastor after pastor had glimpsed spiritual multiplication, and they were ready to see how their entire city could be confronted with the claims of Christ.

When the Here's Life, Singapore campaign was over, I realized that what God had done in that one city alone far exceeded what many expected to see happen through all of Here's Life, Asia! And yet, this was only the beginning of what He planned to do through this city saturation program.

It was becoming obvious by this time that we needed a very capable person to coordinate, develop and implement the Here's Life strategy across Asia. I was busily looking for this individual until one day the Lord impressed me that he was right under my nose! My administrator, John Cragin, had already proved a very gifted assistant with Here's Life, Asia, and he accepted responsibility of heading up the Here's Life, Asia Task Force. Since then John has transferred to another assignment in our ministry, but in the interim God brought to us a man equally as gifted in the person of Jerry Sharpless. Jerry brought with him very valuable experience from his involvement with Here's Life, America, and he is now traveling nearly non-stop across the Orient, helping implement this key strategy.

Through the success in Singapore, Manila and other cities, the Here's Life strategy gained wide acceptance and continued to develop. We were still learning many lessons during the initial campaigns in major cities. At this time, we had some 550 Asian staff ministering in 25 countries. We began to wonder, "With so few staff members, how can we train the

A Spiritual Epidemic 123

" . . . never-ending rural villages, where the pages of history are turned back hundreds of years."

Villages like this one in the Philippines house 80% of the population of Asia.

" . . . a solid, concrete plan of evangelism and spiritual multiplication centered in the churches."

Here's Life, Singapore volunteers man the phones.

number of people necessary to implement our strategy?"

Faced with the same problem, the United States ministry had developed a "mediated training package" employing various forms of media — automatic slide projectors, 16mm color films of Dr. Bright's messages on the Spirit-filled life, etc. But from the Asian perspective, production costs for such a package were prohibitive. We would need thousands of such units in at least 50 languages to saturate the Asian population, which is over 60% of the total world population.

And yet, as we analyzed the situation, we knew that mediated training was the answer to providing quality, effective training. So we began to ask God for His wisdom to know how to reduce the cost to a bare minimum. God's solution, timely and perfect as always, enabled a group of us who were all inexperienced in media to put together a mediated training package for Asia at a fraction of the cost of those produced in North America.

Through the use of colored filmstrips and audio cassettes, we assembled a unit containing five 30-minute messages on the ministry of the Holy Spirit, a message entitled "How to Be Sure You Are a Christian," an evangelistic message entitled "The Greatest Story Ever Told," and six one-hour training seminars. Included are a filmstrip machine, tape recorder, speaker, amplification system and an attractive carrying case — all for $150 in U.S. dollars!

After the original units were produced, some men with media expertise helped us improve the quality of the entire package without raising the cost. It has been one of the major blessings in my recent years to see those units completed at a cost we could afford, and in time to use during our Here's Life movement across Asia. We hardly knew what we were doing, and time was running out — but God's hand guided us in every step.

Once we'd produced mediated training models in English, our next priority was to translate them into 21 languages. This process required careful interpretation so that the messages and concepts communicated to people in their respective cultures.

At this point God also provided staff and equipment for a modern photographic laboratory in our headquarters which is probably the only one of its kind in the Orient. These facilities

A Spiritual Epidemic

enabled us to produce filmstrips of the highest quality at the lowest possible prices. Trained personnel in our U.S. ministry came to set up this facility and train additional people to staff it.

When these mediated training packages were made available, Spirit-filled pastors and laymen began to see the possibilities of exposing millions to the gospel within days. As a result, the Here's Life strategy began to spread from city to city, with little prompting on the part of our staff.

In both Malaysia and Taiwan (Republic of China), Here's Life was launched in the capital cities of Kuala Lumpur (Malaysia) and Taipei (Taiwan). We planned for these two major cities to serve as models for their nation, so that later Here's Life would eventually spread to the rest of the country.

The Lord had other plans. Shortly after we launched Here's Life in the two capitals, pastors from other major cities in Malaysia and Taiwan began to ask, "Why not our cities as well?" The momentum had begun, and pastors and laymen had caught a vision of what Here's Life could do in their own cities. They wanted to begin now!

It was spreading like wildfire. Little did I dream by the time the media campaign began in Kuala Lumpur, seven principal cities of Malaysia would be conducting their campaigns simultaneously! And in Taiwan, the 15 largest cities woke up with 我找到了！(I found it!) spread across their cities on the same day Taipei did! God did a mighty work in both those nations as Christians who were eager to find a way to reach their fellow countrymen got involved.

Just look at what the Lord did in the country of Malaysia, which is under Islamic control. Laws restrict Christian activity among the Malays, who make up half of the population. But through the united efforts of Christians to reach the other 40% (mostly Chinese), God overcame these and other barriers intended to stop the campaign. During the first two weeks of the campaign, 11,773 inquirers heard the gospel through campaign workers from 99 participating churches. Another 40,000 people in all responded to the media campaign.

The Here's Life, Kuala Lumpur staff tell me that 3,507 individuals indicated that they received Christ. A total of 1,797, or more than 50%, enrolled in follow-up Bible studies in the churches, and 30 days after the campaign, attendance increased an average of nine people per church in the 370 churches participating across the nation. A month later, attendance was up 20% in these churches!

In Taiwan, pastor after pastor told me they had never seen such close cooperation among different denominations. Response was far greater than anticipated, with the Taipei media campaign alone producing over 64,000 media responses. Some 7,500 trained campaign workers from 100 churches in Taipei shared the gospel with more than 11,000 of these, and saw 4,783 invite Jesus Christ to come into their lives.

Participating Chinese pastors were increasingly positive. "I had 30 people trained in my church," said Mr. Chiu Kung-Ming, of Min-Shen Baptist Church. "In the first week of the Here's Life campaign, these workers contacted 210 people and 60 prayed and received Christ. As a result, we've set up 10 Bible study classes. Our work has just begun!"

That perspective is still true today, as the "I found it!" campaign continues across the Orient. It was August of 1975 when the idea of Here's Life, Asia was conceived. By October of 1978, Here's Life model cities were developed in almost every country of Asia and the South Pacific where governmental regulations would allow the churches to carry out such a strategy.

In the spring of 1978, the "I found it!" campaign in Hong Kong was described by a major secular newspaper as "a record-breaker in every way." Certainly it was one of the most fruitful, successful thrusts for the gospel that we have seen anywhere. Trained campaign workers numbered 15,000, while another 85,000 believers participated in other ways. These 100,000 Christians — representing about half of the colony's Protestant population — came from 359 participating churches.

During the media campaign, the gospel was presented to 87,174 persons, and 28,174 indicated decisions to trust Christ. Of these new Christians, 10,418 enrolled in Bible studies and youth fellowships. One month after the campaign, 200 of the participating churches reported growth in attendance of between 30 to 150 each, and several had started branch churches.

Surveys showed that 85% of Hong Kong's 4.5 million residents were made aware of the "I found it!" phrase during the 17-day media campaign. I believe that prayer truly paved the way for this thrust, because 5,000 prayer cells consisting of three or four Christians each were formed four months before the campaign. One of the most moving scenes I have ever witnessed occurred near the end of the campaign, when scores of former Buddhists living in Hong Kong's high-rise apartments brought their idols and altars down to a central courtyard and burned them publicly!

Apart from the first 25 cities, Here's Life has been launched in Hong Kong; Colombo, Sri Lanka; Tirunelveli and Bangalore, India; Bangkok, Thailand; Jakarta, Indonesia; Nagoya, Japan; Macau; and Cebu, Iloilo, Bacolod and Cabanatuan, Philippines.

Through this movement, established churches are growing rapidly, and new churches are being planted. Congregations of many denominations have started working together in a united effort to help reach their city, country and eventually the world for Christ.

Here's Life, Asia is not a human accomplishment. But people were willing to invest their time, energy, finances, imagination and intellect in the fulfillment of God's greatest desire, rather than their own.

Personal Application

Would you be honest with me for a moment? Before God, think through the way you have used your time, energy, finances, imagination and intellect over the past month.

Did you invest them in helping to fulfill God's greatest desire — giving every person He created an opportunity to respond to His love and forgiveness made known through Jesus Christ?

Or are you letting your resources slip through your fingers, spent on the fulfillment of your own desires and goals?

The decision to become actively involved in the fulfillment of the Great Commission is yours. I can only assure you that the privilege of being a channel of God's blessing and power has become for me the most thrilling adventure I can experience. Discover this same adventure as you invest your life and your resources, in a very deliberate sense, in telling the good news of our Lord Jesus Christ.

CHAPTER FOURTEEN

The Family Business

I had never seen such overwhelming physical agony in my life. As I walked through that Vietnamese army hospital in Saigon, following my missionary friend from one overcrowded ward to another, I could hardly believe my eyes.

Even more than the patients' mutilated bodies, I saw the void look in their eyes — and I sensed an even deeper agony of their spirits. My heart cried out to tell them how much God loved them, but because of the language barrier all I could do was smile at them.

I stopped at the bed of a boy about 16 years old. One of his legs had been amputated, and from the looks of the bandages on the other, perhaps he would lose it as well. His eyes seemed to beg me for help.

I stood there and prayed, asking God to let me somehow tell this young fellow about Jesus. I held up before his face a Vietnamese Four Spiritual Laws booklet, pointing to the cover sentence, "Have you heard of the Four Spiritual Laws?" The lad shook his head to indicate that he hadn't.

Holding the book before him and moving my finger under each line, I said the English to myself silently. At the same time, I was praying for him. When we reached the circles representing two kinds of lives, he indicated that the circle on the left (without Christ) represented his life. He read the next question and nodded that he wanted the circle on the right (with Christ) to represent his life.

We went to the next page, and he read through the prayer of faith. Using my finger, I asked the question, "Does this prayer express the desire of your heart?" He nodded once again, and excitement was visible in his eyes and mine as well! That young fellow had received Christ into his life by faith, and I hadn't even opened my mouth! When we finished, I gave him one copy of all the Vietnamese materials I had and walked on through the ward.

Some minutes later, my unbelief got the best of me. I kept arguing with myself, "This is not real. Could it really be true?

He didn't really understand . . . or did he?" I couldn't leave without some assurance, so I returned to his bedside.

When I came up the second time, he still had the Four Spiritual Laws booklet in his hand, studying over the circle diagrams. As he looked up and saw me, he smiled. Pointing at the circle without Christ, he shook his head negatively. Then, pointing at the circle with Christ in the life, he nodded his head as if to say "yes" and touched his chest.

Assured that Christ was in his life, I stood by his bed with tears running down my cheeks. The look of pain and despair in his eyes had been replaced with a peaceful look of hope.

What a difference Christ makes . . .

* * *

Nations consist of people — some young, some old, from all walks of life. In a ministry such as ours, it would be easy for me to get caught up with big plans on a national scale, or from the continental perspective, and forget the ordinary man on the street.

But God keeps reminding me of His perspective: in order for nations to be reached, individuals must be reached.

Jesus said that the angels of God rejoice when one person receives Christ (Luke 15:10)! So I never get tired of hearing stories about "just one individual" who responded to the claims of Christ. I actually get thrilled all over again at the transformation God has brought to my own life, and I am reminded of the apostle Paul's comment in II Corinthians 5:17:

> "When someone becomes a Christian, he becomes a brand new person inside. He is not the same any more. A new life has begun!" (LB).

Since we have been living in Asia, Elizabeth and I have had the great privilege of watching such a transformation take place right in our own family.

Our youngest child, Rebecca (known to most as Becca), was born during our first year in Singapore. Like many a child of missionary parents, she grew up surrounded by the gospel. People around her were always talking about Jesus, so by the time Becca was four years old, she could discuss intelligently with anyone Christ's birth, life, death, resurrection and ascension.

The Family Business

Therefore, we were quite amazed when Becca refused various opportunities to receive Christ, repeating with growing stubbornness, "I'm not ready yet." After awhile, she added the statement, "I'm going to wait until I'm eight years old."

Then one morning, while Becca was drinking a cup of hot chocolate next door with Mrs. Newbold, the subject of the second coming of Christ came up. Mrs. Newbold asked, "Becca, what do you think will happen when Christ does come again?"

Becca repeated what she had been taught, that the Christians would go to meet Christ. Mrs. Newbold then inquired, "Well, who around here, in your house and mine, are Christians?"

Becca proceeded to name everyone in both houses except for herself. As the sequence continued, Becca finally realized that she would be the only one left if Christ were to come that day.

"Well, what are you going to do, Becca?" Mrs. Newbold asked.

After a short silence, Becca said, "Maybe Christ will wait until I am eight years old."

We agreed as a family not to pressure her, realizing that a real struggle was going on in her little heart. Then one day she began to tell others that she was already a Christian! She announced that this had happened at EXPLO '74. We knew that this was not true, because although Becca had gone to Korea with us during EXPLO '74, she simply enjoyed reminding her big sister and brother that she had taken a trip without them. We continued to pray for her and read her Bible stories, encouraging other staff and friends to do the same.

One evening after school when Becca was five, she was pestering her big sister while Lisa did her homework. On the edge of Lisa's desk was Dr. Bright's booklet, "How to Be Sure You Are a Christian." Becca asked what the words said on the front of the book, so Lisa read them to her. Then she asked quietly, "Becca, are you sure you are a Christian?"

It was like turning on a record, "Oh yes, I'm a Christian," said Becca. "I invited Christ into my life at EXPLO '74."

Wisely, Lisa said, "Becca, tell me how it happened."

"Well," said Becca, thinking fast, "one afternoon in the hotel, I was all alone. So I got out the Bible and began to read it. Then I invited Christ to come into my life."

Lisa looked down at her baby sister, 10 years her junior, and shook her head gently. "Becca, you can't read."

Becca's defenses collapsed, and Lisa continued, "Wouldn't you like to invite Christ to come into your heart right now?"

With a sigh of relief, Becca replied, "Yes, Lis, I would." So she bowed her blond head there with Lisa and asked Jesus Christ to come into her life to be her Lord and Savior.

Elizabeth and I were away traveling at the time, but when we returned home, Becca bounded out the front door, yelling her happy announcement, "I'm a Christian now! Jesus Christ is in my heart!" We could see that a new birth had taken place in our little girl's life, and she was clearly "under new management"! Oh, she's still very much a little girl, and still in possession of a sin nature — but to see what the Spirit of God has done and continues to do in her heart has been one of the most beautiful experiences that Elizabeth and I have shared.

About a year later, Becca asked me to bring a Four Spiritual Laws picture-book home from the office. This is a booklet developed in Asia to help poor readers and illiterates understand the gospel. I had shown it to Becca while we were still developing it, so she was familiar with the book. When I gave it to her, I asked why she wanted it. She explained that there were some very bad little boys in her first grade class at school who needed to become Christians. Saying nothing more, I gave her the booklet.

For a number of days the booklet went back and forth to school in her lunch box, until I forgot about it. But one day when Elizabeth picked up Becca after school, her teacher ran over and said, "Mrs. Marks, let me tell you what happened in school today."

The teacher, who had come to Christ through one of our staff, explained that shortly before recess, she'd seen Becca sitting in the back of the room talking to one of the little boys. She walked in their direction out of curiosity, only to hear this six-year-old child sharing Christ with her fellow student! The teacher asked Becca to share the booklet with the entire class.

So Becca assembled them all in a little group so they could see the pictures, and she proceeded to explain, "God loves you and has a wonderful plan for your life. But you are sinful and separated from God because of your sin. However, because of God's love, Jesus Christ came and died on the cross for your sins."

Then Becca very "tactfully" informed them that if they did not want to go to hell, they should pray and invite Christ to come into their lives! After this rather direct approach, the teacher reported that all of her students except one indicated they had asked Jesus to come into their hearts. I don't know who was more excited that day — Elizabeth or Becca's teacher!

As far as we know, no one ever told Rebecca that she needed to share the love of Christ with her friends. But God's Spirit had impressed that responsibility upon her, and already she had begun the pattern of sharing Christ as a way of life. Nothing could please her parents more!

What a thrill it is for Elizabeth and me to watch all three of our children mature spiritually through the years. Our older two, now Christian teenagers, find opportunity frequently to confront their classmates and friends with the claims of Christ. At the Brent High School where they are enrolled in Baguio City, the Philippines, they often turn the question, "What does your father do?" into a springboard for conversations about Jesus.

Lisa has followed in her mother's footsteps in wanting to minister to teenage girls. When a high school freshman, she organized a Coke party with Elizabeth's help, in order to show "Life Is Where I'm Going," an evangelistic film our ministry had recently completed. After my wife gave her testimony and explained how to receive Christ, all but one of the 12 girls responded to invite Christ into their lives. One of the girls told Lisa, "I've gone to church all my life, but this is the first time it ever made sense!"

Out of that group, weekly discipleship classes began in our home — first taught by Elizabeth, and then branching out as Lisa learned to lead her own groups. My wife also maintains a very active ministry with U.S. military wives, along with her involvement on a national scale with various national and international Christian leaders. And yet, throughout her varied and ever-growing ministry, God always keeps a very warm spot in Elizabeth's heart for her teenagers.

Bailey, Jr., also actively shares his faith, and nothing thrills me more as I return home from my various ministry trips than to sit down with him and hear his reports of the "divine appointments" the Lord has given him to tell others about Jesus. Among these he has had the privilege to lead to Christ his guitar teacher, a young man in his early twenties.

How thankful I am that Elizabeth and I are not the only ones in our family involved in the fulfillment of the Great Commission — our children have gotten into the "family business" in a wonderful way!

Personal Application

My travel agent tells me that I log approximately 100,000 miles per year as I continually crisscross the Orient, helping to fulfill the Great Commission in this part of the world. However, I believe that after my responsibility to God Himself, my first priority is the spiritual building and discipling of my own family. That means that the greatest thing I can do, as Asia-South Pacific director of affairs for our ministry, is to minister directly and by example in the lives of my wife and three children.

Is your vision greatly expanded for the worldwide fulfillment of the Great Commission? If so, I rejoice, but I caution you: don't ever lose sight of the individuals, the ordinary people with whom you rub shoulders every day. The place to begin a ministry is with your own family.

CHAPTER FIFTEEN

High Dividends

"Look around you! Vast fields of human souls are ripening all around us, and are ready now for reaping. The reapers . . . will be gathering eternal souls into the granaries of heaven!" (John 4:35,36, LB).

You don't have to travel through the nations of the Orient to see the great spiritual harvest fields which our Savior pointed out to the disciples.

Today the whole world seems to be opening up and responding to the spread of the gospel — even areas that have been closed for centuries! Muslims in the Middle East, as well as in Indonesia and other parts of the world, are turning to Christ in faith and commitment. Significant numbers of Hindus in India, Buddhists in Japan, and Animists in Africa, Latin America and tribal areas of Asia are coming to know Christ. In the Western World, tens of thousands from nominal Christian backgrounds are admitting that in their religion they have nothing more than a code of ethics, and they are committing their lives to the person of Jesus Christ.

God is at work in an unusual way all over the world. But we face the same problem that Jesus identified to His disciples: "The harvest is so great, and the workers are so few. So pray to the one in charge of the harvesting, and ask Him to recruit more workers for His harvest fields" (Matthew 9:37, LB). Our Lord stressed 2,000 years ago that "we need laborers." That continues to be true in our own generation.

It is true that revolutionary forms of government threaten to destroy the world as we know it today. Moral and spiritual decay is evident everywhere. But in the very presence of this threat, we must not miss a glorious fact: *Today we have more freedom to preach the gospel than ever before in the history of mankind*! In addition, we have never had more ways and means through media and technology, as well as various forms of rapid transportation, to reach all of mankind in a very short period of time. We cannot afford to wait any longer!

If we as the children of God are to address ourselves seriously to the fulfillment of the Great Commission in our generation, we must confront the issue of total commitment. I have discovered over the past few years that any call for total commitment to Jesus Christ seems to raise the very same barriers for people — whether they are young or old, in one country or another, regardless of culture or background. In fact, from a passage found in Mark 1:16-20, it appears to me that the problem is at least 2,000 years old:

> "Now as He walked by the Sea of Galilee, He saw Simon and Andrew, his brother, casting a net into the sea; for they were fishers. And Jesus said unto them, Come after me, and I will make you become fishers of men. And straightway *they forsook their nets*, and followed Him. And when He had gone a little farther, He saw James, the son of Zebedee, and John, his brother, who also were in the boat mending their nets. And straightway He called them; and *they left their father*, Zebedee, in the boat with hired servants, and went after Him" (KJV) (Italics mine).

Take note of the two phrases in italics: *they forsook their nets* and *they left their father*. I believe these factors represent two of the greatest barriers which every individual faces in making a total commitment of his or her life to God:

1. What will my family think or do?
2. What about my business . . . or the security of my family and future?

The disciples had to place their love for Christ and their commitment to Him above their ability to earn money and above their family relationships. This does not mean that they loved their father or family less, but it does mean that they loved the Lord more. Total commitment calls for nothing less.

When you are living a life filled with the Holy Spirit, in the center of God's will, you will be experiencing all He has to offer — the abundant life He promised. As a matter of spiritual inventory, I would like for you to answer these four questions:

1. Do I desire to be in the center of God's will for my life?
2. Am I willing to go anywhere that God leads me, and do anything that He asks me to do?
3. Am I willing to stay right where I am, if this is what He wants for my life?
4. Am I willing to spend my life in total obedience to the

Great Commission, as an expression of my love and trust for Christ?

An honest "yes" to each of these questions is not easy. Wholehearted abandon to the fulfillment of the Great Commission means that you trust the Lord enough to commit a major portion of your daily life to this cause.

What amount of time are you willing to give to the Lord? Will you give 20, 30, 40, 50 or 100% of your time to this goal? Tens of thousands of Christians are needed to forsake all and follow Him, committing their lives to serving the Lord in a full-time capacity. Every skill is needed, along with the experience of age and the enthusiasm of youth. God wants ordinary people, like you and me.

He wants *you* — not your neighbor, or your pastor — but *you*, in the perfect center of His will, filled with the Holy Spirit, prepared to do whatever He desires of you. Once you are there, He will reveal exactly what He wants you to do. He may not want you to go anywhere, knowing that you can be used most effectively right where you are. On the other hand, He may want you to get up and go to the other side of the world.

When our Lord met a group of ordinary fishermen who were available, He took them and turned them into extraordinary people. Those men had no idea what was in store for the rest of their lives — the close relationships to be developed, the hard lessons to be learned, the inexpressible joy that would be theirs, and the revolutionary, permanent impact they would make on the world. They didn't even ask Jesus what their job descriptions would be. They just dropped their nets and joined Him.

They were ordinary men, ready and available, and they stepped out to follow Jesus. In the course of their lives, they learned to be obedient to God, and consequently, they became extraordinary men.

I am still learning those simple lessons — to be available to God, to learn obedience, to glimpse more and more of God's wonderful plan for my life in reaching the world. While I live on this earth, I want to experience everything God has in store for me — I don't want to find out in heaven that I missed parts of the rich, abundant life through my disobedience. And at the close of my life, I want to be able to say with the apostle Paul,

"I did not prove disobedient to the heavenly vision ..." (Acts 26:19).

Could there be a greater commitment, with higher dividends, for *your* life?

Have You Heard of the Four Spiritual Laws?

Just as there are physical laws that govern the physical universe, so are there spiritual laws which govern your relationship with God.

LAW ONE

GOD **LOVES** YOU, AND OFFERS A WONDERFUL **PLAN** FOR YOUR LIFE.

(References should be read in context from the Bible wherever possible.)

God's Love

"For God so loved the world, that He gave His only begotten Son, that whoever believes in Him should not perish, but have eternal life" (John 3:16).

God's Plan

(Christ speaking) "I came that they might have life, and might have it abundantly" (that it might be full and meaningful) (John 10:10).

Why is it that most people are not experiencing the abundant life?

Because . . .

LAW TWO

MAN IS **SINFUL** and **SEPARATED** FROM GOD. THEREFORE, HE CANNOT KNOW AND EXPERIENCE GOD'S LOVE AND PLAN FOR HIS LIFE.

Man Is Sinful

"For all have sinned and fall short of the glory of God" (Romans 3:23).

Man was created to have fellowship with God; but, because of his stubborn self-will, he chose to go his own independent way and fellowship with God was broken. This self-will, characterized by an attitude of active rebellion or passive indifference, is evidence of what the Bible calls sin.

Man Is Separated

"For the wages of sin is death" (spiritual separation from God) (Romans 6:23).

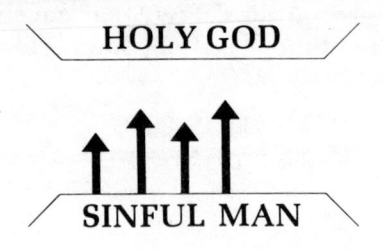

```
\   HOLY GOD   /
    ↑ ↑ ↑
/  SINFUL MAN  \
```

This diagram illustrates that God is holy and man is sinful. A great gulf separates the two. The arrows illustrate that man is continually trying to reach God and the abundant life through his own efforts, such as a good life, philosophy or religion.

The third law explains the only way to bridge this gulf . . .

LAW THREE

JESUS CHRIST IS GOD'S **ONLY** PROVISION FOR MAN'S SIN. THROUGH HIM YOU CAN KNOW AND EXPERIENCE GOD'S LOVE AND PLAN FOR YOUR LIFE.

He Died in Our Place

"But God demonstrates His own love toward us, in that while we were yet sinners, Christ died for us" (Romans 5:8).

He Rose from the Dead

"Christ died for our sins . . . He was buried . . . He was raised on the third day, according to the Scriptures . . . He appeared to Peter, then to the twelve. After that He appeared to more than five hundred . . ." (I Corinthians 15:3-6).

He Is the Only Way to God

"Jesus said to him, 'I am the way, and the truth, and the life; no one comes to the Father, but through Me'" (John 14:6).

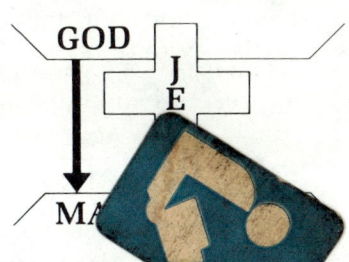

This diagram illustrates that God has bridged the gulf which separates us from God by sending His Son, Jesus Christ, to die on the cross in our place to pay the penalty for our sins.

It is not enough just to know these three laws . . .

LAW FOUR

WE MUST INDIVIDUALLY **RECEIVE** JESUS CHRIST AS SAVIOR AND LORD; THEN WE CAN KNOW AND EXPERIENCE GOD'S LOVE AND PLAN FOR OUR LIVES.

We Must Receive Christ

"But as many as received Him, to them He gave the right to become children of God, even to those who believe in His name" (John 1:12).

We Receive Christ through Faith

"For by grace you have been saved through faith; and that not of yourselves, it is the gift of God; not as a result of works, that no one should boast" (Ephesians 2:8, 9).

When We Receive Christ, We Experience a New Birth

(Read John 3:1-8).

We Receive Christ by Personal Invitation

(Christ is speaking) "Behold, I stand at the door and knock; if any one hears My voice and opens the door, I will come in to him" (Revelation 3:20).

Receiving Christ involves turning from self to God (repentance) and trusting Christ to come into our lives to forgive our sins and to make us the kind of person He wants us to be. Just to agree intellectually that Jesus Christ is the Son of God and that He died on the cross for our sins is not enough. Nor is it enough to have an emotional experience. We receive Jesus Christ by faith, as an act of the will.

These two circles represent two kinds of lives:

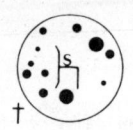

SELF-DIRECTED LIFE
S—Self on the throne
†—Christ is outside the life
•—Interests are directed by self, often resulting in discord and frustration

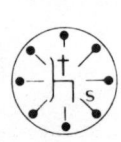

CHRIST-DIRECTED LIFE
†—Christ is in the life
S—Self is yielding to Christ
•—Interests are directed by Christ, resulting in harmony with God's plan

Which circle best represents your life?

Which circle would you like to have represent your life?

The following explains how you can receive Christ:

YOU CAN RECEIVE CHRIST RIGHT NOW BY FAITH THROUGH PRAYER

(Prayer is talking with God)

God knows your heart and is not so concerned with your words as He is with the attitude of your heart. The following is a suggested prayer:

"Lord Jesus, I need You. Thank You for dying on the cross for my sins. I open the door of my life and receive You as my Savior and Lord. Thank You for forgiving my sins and giving me eternal life. Make me the kind of person You want me to be."

Does this prayer express the desire of your heart?

If it does, pray this prayer right now, and Christ will come into your life, as He promised.

Have You Made the Wonderful Discovery of the Spirit-filled Life?

EVERY DAY CAN BE AN EXCITING ADVENTURE FOR THE CHRISTIAN who knows the reality of being filled with the Holy Spirit and who lives constantly, moment by moment, under His gracious direction.

The Bible tells us that there are three kinds of people:

1. NATURAL MAN
(One who has not received Christ)

"But a natural man does not accept the things of the Spirit of God; for they are foolishness to him, and he cannot understand them, because they are spiritually appraised" (I Corinthians 2:14).

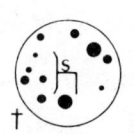

SELF-DIRECTED LIFE
- S—Ego or finite self is on the throne
- †—Christ is outside the life
- •—Interests are directed by self, often resulting in discord and frustration

2. SPIRITUAL MAN
(One who is directed and empowered by the Holy Spirit)

"But he who is spiritual appraises all things . . ." (I Corinthians 2:15).

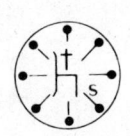

CHRIST-DIRECTED LIFE
- †—Christ is in the life and on the throne
- S—Self is yielding to Christ
- •—Interests are directed by Christ, resulting in harmony with God's plan

3. CARNAL MAN
(One who has received Christ, but who lives in defeat because he trusts in his own efforts to live the Christian life)

"And I, brethren, could not speak to you as to spiritual

men, but as to carnal men, as to babes in Christ. I gave you milk to drink, not solid food; for you were not yet able to receive it. Indeed, even now you are not yet able, for you are still carnal. For since there is jealousy and strife among you, are you not fleshly, and are you not walking like mere men?" (I Corinthians 3:1-3).

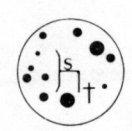

SELF-DIRECTED LIFE
S—Self is on the throne
†—Christ dethroned and not allowed to direct the life
•—Interests are directed by self, often resulting in discord and frustration

1. GOD HAS PROVIDED FOR US AN ABUNDANT AND FRUITFUL CHRISTIAN LIFE.

Jesus said, "I came that they might have life, and might have it abundantly" (John 10:10).

"I am the vine, you are the branches; he who abides in Me, and I in him, he bears much fruit; for apart from Me you can do nothing" (John 15:5).

"But the fruit of the Spirit is love, joy, peace, patience, kindness, goodness, faithfulness, gentleness, self-control; against such things there is no law" (Galatians 5:22,23).

"But you shall receive power when the Holy Spirit has come upon you; and you shall be My witnesses both in Jerusalem, and in all Judea and Samaria, and even to the remotest part of the earth" (Acts 1:8).

THE SPIRITUAL MAN — Some personal traits which result from trusting God:

Christ-centered
Empowered by the Holy Spirit
Introduces others to Christ
Effective prayer life
Understands God's Word
Trusts God
Obeys God

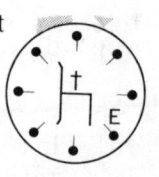

Love
Joy
Peace
Patience
Kindness
Faithfulness
Goodness

The degree to which these traits are manifested in the life depends upon the extent to which the Christian trusts the

The Spirit Filled Life

Lord with every detail of his life, and upon his maturity in Christ. One who is only beginning to understand the ministry of the Holy Spirit should not be discouraged if he is not as fruitful as more mature Christians who have known and experienced this truth for a longer period.

Why is it that most Christians are not experiencing the abundant life?

2. CARNAL CHRISTIANS CANNOT EXPERIENCE THE ABUNDANT AND FRUITFUL CHRISTIAN LIFE.

The carnal man trusts in his own efforts to live the Christian life:

- A. He is either uninformed about, or has forgotten, God's love, forgiveness, and power (Romans 5:8-10; Hebrews 10:1-25; I John 1; 2:1-3; II Peter 1:9; Acts 1:8).
- B. He has an up-and-down spiritual experience.
- C. He cannot understand himself — he wants to do what is right, but cannot.
- D. He fails to draw upon the power of the Holy Spirit to live the Christian life.

(I Corinthians 3:1-3; Romans 7:15-24; 8:7; Galatians 5:16-18)

THE CARNAL MAN — Some or all of the following traits may characterize the Christian who does not fully trust God:

Ignorance of his spiritual heritage
Unbelief
Disobedience
Loss of love for God and for others
Poor prayer life
No desire for Bible study
Legalistic attitude

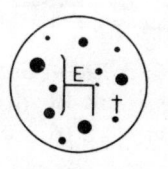

Impure thoughts
Jealousy
Guilt
Worry
Discouragement
Critical spirit
Frustration
Aimlessness

(The individual who professes to be a Christian but who continues to practice sin should realize that he may not be a Christian at all, according to I John 2:3, 3:6, 9; Ephesians 5:5.)

The third truth gives us the only solution to this problem . . .

3. **JESUS PROMISED THE ABUNDANT AND FRUITFUL LIFE AS THE RESULT OF BEING FILLED (DIRECTED AND EMPOWERED) BY THE HOLY SPIRIT.**

The Spirit-filled life is the Christ-directed life by which Christ lives His life in and through us in the power of the Holy Spirit (John 15).

　A. One becomes a Christian through the ministry of the Holy Spirit, according to John 3:1-8. From the moment of spiritual birth, the Christian is indwelt by the Holy Spirit at all times (John 1:12; Colossians 2:9, 10; John 14:16, 17). **Though all Christians are indwelt by the Holy Spirit, not all Christians are filled (directed and empowered) by the Holy Spirit.**

　B. The Holy Spirit is the source of the overflowing life (John 7:37-39).

　C. The Holy Spirit came to glorify Christ (John 16:1-15). When one is filled with the Holy Spirit, he is a true disciple of Christ.

　D. In His last command before His ascension, Christ promised the power of the Holy Spirit to enable us to be witnesses for Him (Acts 1:1-9).

How, then, can one be filled with the Holy Spirit?

4. **WE ARE FILLED (DIRECTED AND EMPOWERED) BY THE HOLY SPIRIT BY FAITH; THEN WE CAN EXPERIENCE THE ABUNDANT AND FRUITFUL LIFE WHICH CHRIST PROMISED TO EACH CHRISTIAN.**

You can appropriate the filling of the Holy Spirit **right now** if you:

　A. Sincerely desire to be directed and empowered by the Holy Spirit (Matthew 5:6; John 7:37-39).

　B. Confess your sins.

　　By **faith** thank God that He **has** forgiven all of your sins — past, present, and future — because Christ died for you (Colossians 2:13-15; I John 1; 2:1-3; Hebrews 10:1-17).

　C. Present every area of your life to God (Romans 12:1, 2).

The Spirit Filled Life

D. By **faith** claim the fullness of the Holy Spirit, according to:
1. HIS COMMAND — Be filled with the Spirit.
"And do not get drunk with wine, for that is dissipation, but be filled with the Spirit" (Ephesians 5:18).
2. HIS PROMISE — He will always answer when we pray according to His will. "And this is the confidence which we have before Him, that, if we ask anything according to His will, He hears us. And if we know that He hears us in whatever we ask, we know that we have the requests which we have asked from Him" (I John 5:14, 15).

Faith can be expressed through prayer . . .

HOW TO PRAY IN FAITH TO BE FILLED WITH THE HOLY SPIRIT

We are filled with the Holy Spirit by **faith** alone. However, true prayer is one way of expressing your faith. The following is a suggested prayer:

"Dear Father, I need You. I acknowledge that I have been directing my own life and that, as a result, I have sinned against You. I thank You that You have forgiven my sins through Christ's death on the cross for me. I now invite Christ to again take His place on the throne of my life. Fill me with the Holy Spirit as You **commanded** me to be filled, and as You **promised** in Your Word that You would do if I asked in faith. I pray this in the name of Jesus. As an expression of my faith, I now thank You for directing my life and for filling me with the Holy Spirit."

Does this prayer express the desire of your heart? If so, bow in prayer and trust God to fill you with the Holy Spirit **right now.**

HOW TO KNOW THAT YOU ARE FILLED (DIRECTED AND EMPOWERED) BY THE HOLY SPIRIT

Did you ask God to fill you with the Holy Spirit? Do you know that you are now filled with the Holy Spirit? On what authority? (On the trustworthiness of God Himself and His Word: Hebrews 11:6; Romans 14:22, 23.)

Do not depend upon feelings. The promise of God's Word, not our feelings, is our authority. The Christian lives by faith (trust) in the trustworthiness of God Himself and His Word. This train diagram illustrates the relationship between **fact** (God and His Word), **faith** (our trust in God and His Word), and **feeling** (the result of our faith and obedience) (John 14:21).

The train will run with or without the caboose. However, it would be futile to attempt to pull the train by the caboose. In the same way, we, as Christians, do not depend upon feelings or emotions, but we place our faith (trust) in the trustworthiness of God and the promises of His Word.

HOW TO WALK IN THE SPIRIT

Faith (trust in God and in His promises) is the only means by which a Christian can live the Spirit-directed life. As you continue to trust Christ moment by moment:

A. Your life will demonstrate more and more of the fruit of the Spirit (Galatians 5:22, 23) and will be more and more conformed to the image of Christ (Romans 12:2; II Corinthians 3:18).

B. Your prayer life and study of God's Word will become more meaningful.

C. You will experience His power in witnessing (Acts 1:8).

D. You will be prepared for spiritual conflict against the world (I John 2:15-17); against the flesh (Galatians 5:16, 17); and against Satan (I Peter 5:7-9; Ephesians 6:10-13).

E. You will experience His power to resist temptation and sin (I Corinthians 10:13; Philippians 4:13; Ephesians 1:19-23; 6:10; II Timothy 1:7; Romans 6:1-16).